D0278852

How Can I Ever **Trust** You Again?

Infidelity:
From Discovery to Recovery
in Seven Steps

ANDREW G. MARSHALL

LIBRARIES
WITHDRAWN FROM ...

B L O O M S B U R Y
LONDON · BERLIN · NEW YORK

LIBRARIES NI	
C700205251	
RONDO	21/01/2010
306.736	£ 12.99
CLL	

First published in Great Britain 2010

Copyright © 2010 by Andrew G. Marshall

The moral right of the author has been asserted

Bloomsbury Publishing Plc
36 Soho Square
London W1D 3QY

Bloomsbury Publishing, London, New York and Berlin

A CIP catalogue record for this book is available from the British Library

ISBN 978 1 4088 0181 9

10 9 8 7 6 5 4 3 2 1

Typeset by Hewer Text UK Ltd, Edinburgh
Printed in Great Britain by Clays Ltd St Ives plc

Mixed Sources
Product group from well-managed
forests and other controlled sources
www.fsc.org Cert no. SGS-COC-2061
© 1996 Forest Stewardship Council
FSC

www.bloomsbury.com/andrewgmarshall

To my agent, Rachel Calder

Thank you for all your advice, support and understanding

Contents

- The eight types of infidelity: Accidental, Cry for help, Self-medication, Don Juan and Doña Juana, Tripod, Retaliatory, Exploratory, Exit.
- How understanding your partner's type can help predict the future.
- New skill: *Confident and productive decision-making*.

Stage Four: Hope   113

- The shortest stage of all and the most precarious, but both the Discoverer and the Discovered begins to believe that their relationship could be saved.
- The importance of celebrating this fragile moment.
- Laying down a foundation for healing: Safety-first living and Reconstructing the affair in your mind.
- The difference between married love and affair love.
- New skill: *Finding a positive out of a negative*.

Stage Five: Attempted Normality   143

- The initial crisis is over but the aftershock can be equally dangerous.
- The two very different approaches to infidelity ('how can we put this behind us if you keep harping on about the past' and 'how can I move on if I don't understand') and how they drive couples apart.
- Why couples snipe and how small things can turn into big arguments.
- Suppression, obsession and hyper-vigilance, the three coping mechanisms that can derail healing.
- New skill: *Looking beneath the surface*.

Introduction

Almost one in five couples who come to my marital counselling office are dealing with the fall-out from an affair. In fact, it is the fourth most common reason for seeking my help. According to the British Sexual Fantasy Research Project, 55 per cent of the adult population have committed adultery at some point; while Kinsey's groundbreaking research in forties and fifties America found that 26 per cent of married women and 50 per cent of married men had cheated on their spouses. Subsequent research has produced similar findings. When you throw in all the couples who have been living together or dating, the numbers are even greater. At times, it feels like a tidal wave of misery, betrayal and hurt is flooding my therapy office.

However, it is not all bad news. Infidelity might be a terrible crisis but the Chinese symbol for crisis is made up of two words: danger and opportunity. If you have bought this book after discovering your partner's adultery or because your own adultery has been discovered and your relationship is hanging in the balance, you will be only too aware of the danger. My aim is to open your eyes to the opportunity. Infidelity turns life upside down and makes you question everything. The fear that it could all happen again shines a spotlight on all the murky corners of your relationship and provides the impetus to change. Sometimes clients moan: 'I just want my old life back.' That's not possible, but if you seize on the opportunity part of crisis, you can find a deeper, more durable and ultimately better relationship.

I have tried to keep the tone of this book compassionate. (There are exceptions, but few people set out to have an affair.) It is mainly aimed at the Discoverers of adultery – because they are generally the most hurt and most in need of answers – but each chapter has a box addressed specifically to the Discovered. My hope is that couples will share the book and find that the exercises provide them with a bridge to understanding each other better. If you are the third party in the affair triangle, you will find less of direct benefit. However, I hope this book will provide an insight into the dynamics of adultery and, if your affair has ended, to help in the healing process.

In writing *How Can I Ever Trust You Again?*, I have drawn on clients from over twenty-five years of marital therapy as well as interviews with people not in counselling and questionnaires filled in by visitors to my website. (This research was publicised in articles about infidelity in several leading UK newspapers and by the *Huffington Post* – the Internet newspaper. In total, fifteen hundred questionnaires were submitted from all over the world. Sixty-eight per cent were completed by people who had discovered their partner's infidelity, 32 per cent by those who had been unfaithful – and of these just over half had confessed to their partner about the affair.) To protect confidentiality, I have blended sometimes two or three cases together. My thanks, as always, to everyone who has shared their experiences. I hope it helped make sense of what happened and provided the building blocks for a brighter future.

How to use this book:

- The main part of each chapter is written for someone who has discovered their partner's infidelity.
- At the end of each chapter, there is a box for people who have been unfaithful. This is followed by a section about the particular lesson from this stage in the journey and a summary of the whole chapter.
- It is better if both you and your partner read the whole book. However, I have designed the programme so that it will work if your partner only reads his or her section.

- Don't worry if your partner distrusts self-help books, or is uncertain about the future; this programme will help *you* cope better, think before acting and become more balanced. This, in turn, will have a positive knock-on effect on your partner's behaviour and enable the two of you to co-operate better.
- Read the whole programme, so that you have a sense of the overall journey, and then concentrate on your particular stage.
- When you are in crisis, depressed or under stress, turn back to the previous chapter. It could be that you have missed some important piece of healing and need to return and complete that stage.
- Take a deep breath. Keep calm. Things will get better.

Stage One:
Shock and Disbelief

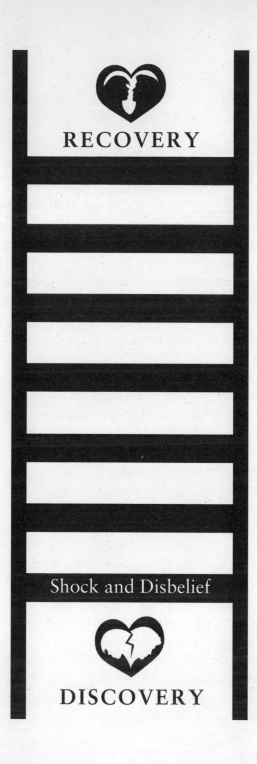

RECOVERY

Shock and Disbelief

DISCOVERY

Good relationships are built on three building blocks: trust, honesty and compassion. We do not need a minute-by-minute breakdown of where our beloved has been or what she or he has done because we *trust* them. If there is a problem, we expect our partner to be *honest* and own up. We hope that the people we love have our best interests at heart and that, when we stumble, they will be *compassionate*. And the wonderful thing about love is that we are prepared to offer the same in return. Under the protection of a good relationship – and trust, honesty and compassion – a couple will not only thrive but also be ready to take on the world. Unfortunately, because these building blocks are so fundamental, we often take them for granted. We seldom even mention trust, honesty and compassion in day-to-day conversation. They are just there, like food, water and shelter. It is only when our partner has been unfaithful, violated our sense of emotional intimacy and destroyed our sense of safety, that we begin to realise how precarious trust, honesty and compassion can be.

If your partner has been unfaithful or you suspect infidelity – or alternatively it is you who have strayed – you will be only too aware of how difficult it is to rebuild a broken relationship. At this point, you will probably fear the damage is irreparable. Perhaps you have neither the desire nor the inclination to try to rebuild the relationship. Trust is at an all-time low and there is probably more anger than compassion. Worst of all, you doubt that you will ever be able to trust your partner, or be trusted, again. However, my message is that not only is it possible to recover from infidelity but it is also possible to come out the other side with a stronger relationship. You will probably feel sceptical, but you will have to take it on trust. There's that word again.

This book is like a journey – from the moment when infidelity is just a vague suspicion that something is not quite right, to discovery, through becoming compassionate towards your partner (and if it is you who have cheated, towards yourself, too), on to being truly honest with each other (equally important whether you are the Discoverer of infidelity or the Discovered) and, ultimately, on to restoring that final and most vital building block: trust. Along the way, there will be doubt, pain and despair but also hope, too. You will discover more about your partner, and yourself, than you ever thought possible. Whatever happens, you will emerge out the other side braver, wiser and stronger.

Naming the unnameable

Before discovering infidelity, there are always tiny moments of suspicion; small flickers that something is wrong and a growing sense of unease. Your partner is repeatedly late back from work, distracted, irritable or on top of the world – all for no discernible reason. He or she seems to be taking a lot of interest in his or her appearance or talking a lot about a particular work colleague. There could be a million reasons for these changes, many of them entirely innocent. In fact, the idea that your partner might be cheating is so unbelievable, so unacceptable that you put the thought away. You start making excuses. You blame work, financial problems and the pressure of small children, teenagers or the kids leaving home. You think 'all relationships go through bad patches' or 'it will get better when the rush at work is over'. You put your head down and soldier on. Unfortunately, relationships can deteriorate so gradually, drip-by-drip, that it is easy to miss how bad things have really become. Therefore, it is often only in retrospect that all the clues make sense.

'My husband would take his mobile phone into the bathroom,' explained Melanie, forty-two, 'I thought it a bit strange – and even the children teased him about it – only later, when I discovered his affair, I realised this was somewhere he could legitimately be alone and text. How could I have been so blind?' When Gregory, thirty-five, discovered his wife taking their child into the wrong entrance of the school, he was puzzled. 'I had forgotten a report, so I had to drive home and collect it. I saw her coming out of the far school gates – at other end of the grounds from our house – which is an extra ten minutes' walk. She's always complaining about being busy, so why go the long way?' When he told his wife, she got defensive and accused him of checking up on her. He let the whole thing drop but later realised that he had witnessed the beginning of the affair. 'She had gone to that entrance in the hope of bumping into the other man.'

Sometimes, it takes someone on the outside to point out the obvious. Even though Karen's husband had been unfaithful in the past and she knew the signs – 'behaving cold, unnaturally tired in the evenings, restless and talking in his sleep' – she did not realise straightaway that his story did not stack up. 'He started to spend at least two days a week away from home, sometimes the weekend too. He told me that he had a big computer job in the Cabinet Office, that he was living in an apartment in Whitehall. His phone had no signal and I should leave a message and he'd ring the following day. It took my youngest brother to point out what a sucker I was being.' With the benefit of hindsight, it seems obvious that these worries were not 'all in the imagination'.

However, there are people who install computer systems in Whitehall and some of them might be asked to work at the weekend. People do suddenly decide to walk a different way to school or have a bath and clear out old contacts from their mobile's address book. To use a detective analogy, these could be red herrings rather than smoking guns. So how can you tell the difference between legitimate worry and being paranoid?

1. *Take the general temperature in your relationship.* How well do you get on, on a daily basis? How easy is it to bring up concerns and share worries? Are you frequently

so pressured that you have little time to listen to your partner? If you compare the atmosphere in the house with the atmosphere twelve months ago, is there a significant difference? If the answers to these questions are worrying, do not jump to conclusions and accuse your partner of adultery. It could be that your early warning system has detected a problem on the horizon. Maybe he or she is developing a 'special friendship' that might still be at the 'innocent' stage and there is time to head the problem off. Going in all guns blazing could put up a barrier between the two of you just when you need to communicate more effectively.

Tip: Set aside more time together, so that there is naturally an opportunity to talk about your relationship or ask your partner whether he or she is happy. This is better than announcing 'we need to talk', which immediately sends some people into panic or defence mode. Ask about stress, how your partner is coping, and whether she or he feels supported. If you truly listen – without rushing to defend yourself or to judge – your partner will not only open up but will also return the favour and listen to your concerns too.

2. *Look at your personal history.* Are there reasons why you find it harder than the average person to trust? Are you generally on your guard? Did your parents get divorced after one of them committed adultery? Has a previous boyfriend or girlfriend let you down badly? Has your partner been unfaithful before? While some people can miss transparently suspect behaviour, there are others who turn even the most innocent conversation with a stranger into first-degree betrayal. It is important to know where you fit on this scale. So ask yourself: do I pump up my fears or do I ignore them? If you are not a naturally suspicious person but your internal alarm bell is ringing,

I would listen to it. If you are like a guard dog – who leaps up because the postman is delivering a parcel three houses away – then think again. (There is more in 'How to reprogram the unnaturally suspicious mind' in the exercise section at the end of this chapter.)

Tip: In many cases, people do have a reason to be anxious. Something is wrong. However, it is not always adultery. It could be that you are tired and feel ignored. It could be that the two of you have not spent much time together lately. So ask directly for what you need – for example: 'Can I have a hug?' – rather than going on the attack and hoping that you can force a moment of tenderness or reassurance out of your partner.

3. *Look at your thought processes.* Do you have a tendency to second-guess and over-analyse? Do you spend hours going over what happened and trying to read between the lines? Do you find it hard to make decisions because you go over all the options so many times that you become overwhelmed and paralysed? If you answer 'yes' to these questions, but in the past have not over-analysed, my guess is that something is wrong. When someone lies, it is very destabilising. With one vital piece of information missing, you will not be able to see the full picture and your head will feel like it is going to explode. However, if you often 'over-think' and put lots of disparate and random facts together to make a cast-iron case, the jury is still out.

Tip: Instead of letting all your thoughts and accusations churn over in your mind – making you more and more anxious, more and more angry – try writing them down instead. On one side of a sheet of paper, list all the 'evidence'. No matter how small, write it down. Next, go back through the list and see if there is anything which now looks irrelevant or overblown. Then go through each

11

surviving item and add the case for the defence. Are there any more items that could be crossed off the list? When I do this exercise with clients, there are normally one or two small but manageable issues to discuss with their partner. (There is more about over-thinking in Stage Five: Attempted Normality.)

4. *Try discussing your general concerns about the relationship with your partner.* What is your partner's reaction when you do talk about specific worries? Is she or he prepared to consider that you have a valid point? Is your partner truly interested in working on your relationship? I once counselled a couple after the husband was caught having an affair. However, whatever I tried, the counselling went nowhere. After six months of mounting frustration and even despair, the wife discovered that her husband had secretly continued the affair. Once the dust had settled, and the affair truly ended, we started again. The atmosphere in my counselling room was transformed in two key ways. Previously, he had been dismissive and aggressive. Second time round, he was prepared to listen and change. If your partner's reaction is overly dismissive or uncharacteristically aggressive, I would be very concerned. If your partner is just defensive, it could be that she or he feels attacked.

Tip: Look at your communication style and check that you do not make a bad situation worse. There are some words that instantly raise the temperature. These tend to be absolute terms like: 'always' and 'never'. (For example, if you say: 'You never tidy up', your partner will list the few times he or she did use the vacuum cleaner.) Avoid other contentious words such as 'keep on', 'must' or 'insist'. Instead, swap them for milder terms such as: 'often' and 'sometimes' or 'like to' and 'prefer'. In this way, you will encourage a debate rather than a row. (There is more under 'Improve your communication style' in the exercise section.)

5. *Keep your eyes open*. If none of these strategies eases your mind, or on the other hand provides incontrovertible evidence, pay particular attention to your partner's behaviour. The next section will explain why he or she might be unconsciously leaving clues.

Tip: Look for behaviour that is out of character and makes you question whether you really know this man or woman. Does she or he suddenly have an interest in something unusual? For example, watching Grand Prix racing on the TV for the first time. Does he or she spout views that you have never heard before? Could they belong to someone else?

If all the signs say your partner is cheating . . .

Most affairs last for an incredibly short time. In my survey on 'Adultery in the UK', 10 per cent had lasted only a few weeks and 40 per cent for less than six months. In most cases, this was because the unfaithful partner had been careless and was quickly discovered. 'I did all these stupid things. I left restaurant receipts in my trouser pockets and a birthday card in the car glove compartment,' explains Julian, forty-three. 'It was only a matter of time before I was discovered. Looking back, I realise I was sabotaging my affair.'

Time and time again, I find that the partner who has been unfaithful might be terrified of the fall-out from discovery but does everything in their power to make certain it happens. Jennifer, thirty-nine, had been married for seven years when she discovered her husband's affair: 'One night during a family holiday, when I think my husband was feeling particularly lonely and separated from his mistress, he told my sister about his affair. She didn't know what to do and told my mother who tried as subtly as she could to encourage me to ask him. Eventually, I did and he categorically denied it and I believed him. Then he continued to bombard me, undermine me and our relationship both in the present and the past. He no longer loved me, he didn't love the children. We were due to have a day out together, without the children, to talk properly but my mother felt it essential that I knew the full story.' It seems amazing that her husband would really expect his sister-in-law to keep his confidence and the truth is, deep down, he probably did not. Subconsciously, he wanted to tell his wife – even though his conscious brain did everything to fight her finding out.

Therefore, if you suspect that your partner is being unfaithful, it is probably because – at some level – he or she wants to be found out. However, I do not advocate turning the house upside down looking for 'evidence'. Instead, talk to your partner about your fears. This direct approach will lay the foundations for honest and open communication – vital if your relationship is going to recover. It also gives your partner an opportunity to be honourable and to make a full confession. This in turn will increase the likelihood of your relationship not only surviving but also thriving. The Travis Research Institute in Pasadena tracked 139 couples, with a variety of problems, through marital therapy. At the start, the couples struggling with infidelity reported the most distress and unhappiness. However, during counselling, the couples where the unfaithful partner had confessed, rather than been found out, made the most progress. What's more, by the end of counselling, they reported the greatest satisfaction with their relationship – greater even than the non-infidelity couples.

How to tackle your partner
Your goal is to take all the things that are currently unsayable, to bring them out into the open and, ultimately, to face them.

1. Plan ahead
- Find a quiet time to talk face-to-face, when you will not be interrupted.
- If you decide to talk away from the house, choose somewhere neutral where you are unlikely to go again.
- If you are someone who procrastinates, set a time limit for tackling your partner.

- Do not blurt out your suspicions in the heat of an argument or on the back of discovering some new piece of incriminating evidence.

2. Think about your approach

- Strategy one is to warm up with a general discussion about your relationship – how it has been going and acknowledging recent problems – before introducing your fears about adultery.
- Strategy two is to ask straight out. Make certain it is a genuine question ('Is there someone else in your life?' or 'Are you having an affair?') rather than an accusation ('You must be cheating' or 'I know you're lying'). Questions invite a discussion. Accusations invite a fight.

3. Be ready with supplementary questions

- In interviews with politicians, and other slippery characters, it is always the follow-up questions that elicit the most information. Some examples would be: 'Have you been talking a lot to someone about your problems?', 'Are you calling or emailing someone a lot?', 'Is anyone becoming more than a friend?' or 'Have you kissed or cuddled someone else?'
- Questions that could elicit your partner's opinions about your relationship could include: 'Why do you find it hard to talk about your problems to me?', 'How could we improve our communication?' or 'Why have we drifted apart?'

4. Ask calmly

- This is the most important element for successfully tackling your partner.
- In flight or fight mode, you will not be able to think straight or ask appropriate follow-up questions.
- Being calm will also stop you going on the attack and your partner raising her or his defences. It will also provide enough detachment for the next point.

5. *Listen to what's behind the response*

- Does your partner's rebuttal seem over the top? For example: 'I would never, ever do something as nasty and sneaky as that.' Especially when a simple 'no' or genuine puzzlement would have been more appropriate. Your partner is trying to hide behind being a moral person and therefore deflect suspicion.
- Does your partner pull in examples from friends or people whose behaviour is worse? In these circumstances, your partner is uncomfortable about something and using other people's failings to make himself or herself look better.
- Does your partner provide reassurance about something that you've not asked? For example, you ask: 'Why have you been so preoccupied?' But your partner replies: 'You know how I feel about lying.'
- Does the answer seem 'off-pat', as if your partner has been expecting your question and has already practised the response a hundred times?
- Listen out for phrases like 'to be perfectly frank', 'to be honest', 'would I lie to you?' and 'to tell the truth'. If they are not normally in your partner's vocabulary, they are all signs that he or she is trying to deflect your attention from what is really going on.

6. *Look at the body language*

- Does your partner have trouble maintaining eye contact? If she or he is forever glancing away, this would indicate lying. Someone who has been falsely accused will lock eyes to try and convince you of their innocence.
- Do your partner's hands keep flying up to his or her face? This is another unconscious signalling of a lie. It is almost as if the hands are trying to hide or screen the mouth.
- Is your partner's body stiff and are their movements hesitant? Do they seem like an unpolished politician or an actor on the TV? This is because when we are relaxed our bodies are relaxed too and our movement is fluid

and natural. When we are trying to hide something, we freeze up.

7. *Lay out the grounds for your suspicion*
- Remembering to keep calm, go through the recent events that seem odd.
- Do not inflate the evidence or link random facts to jump to a conclusion.
- Ask your partner what conclusions she or he would draw.
- If you have anything solid – like a credit-card or phone statement – put that on the table and ask for their comments: 'Why have you called the same number ninety times in the last month?'

8. *Offer a 'carrot' to your partner to confess*
- By this point, if you have been calm and logical, your partner will probably have confessed.
- If your partner is not forthcoming, he or she might need a little help over the final hurdle.
- So offer the 'carrot' of understanding her or his position: 'I know it's tough', 'You don't want to hurt me' or 'You don't want to make things worse.'
- Follow up with another incentive to confess: 'You will feel better if you get it off your chest', 'For me, being in the dark is the most painful place to be' or 'Until we can face the truth, nothing will change.'
- Finally, appeal to your partner's better judgement: 'It will be worse if I find out later that you have lied to me today.'

9. *Don't get embroiled in a row*
- For some partners, the best form of defence is attack. So your partner might accuse you of being paranoid, mad, sneaky, violating his or her privacy, or even cheating yourself.
- It is very easy to get side-tracked and start defending yourself. However, in the heat of a row, you are unlikely to get to the truth.

- Worse still, you could lose the moral high ground and start name-calling or indulging in other hurtful behaviour. In some cases, cheating partners even engineer this kind of row so that they can 'justify' their infidelity to themselves.
- If you feel your internal thermometer heading towards boiling point, or your partner looks likely to blow his or her top, walk away for ten minutes or so. You can talk again when you have both calmed down.

10. Return to the original question
- Sometimes twenty-four hours, and the opportunity to reflect, will make your partner decide to confess.
- So follow up the original discussion by asking: 'I really want to know the truth. Have you been, or are you being, unfaithful?'

Other ways of discovering the truth
Confronting your partner calmly will work with the vast majority of people; however, there are always the exceptions. Here are some alternative strategies and stories from my casebook.

Turning detective
At first sight, this method seems straightforward. However, sometimes all the evidence in the world is not enough. Ellie, twenty-six, was suspicious when her partner came home with a love bite. 'He told me it was a bruise from when he had been working on his car. For some reason, I bought this excuse even though deep down it sounded ridiculous.' Like a lot of cornered partners, Ellie's husband became angry and accused her of being paranoid. 'I was pregnant at the time and he also blamed my hormones,' she explained. Next, Ellie found videos of this woman on his laptop. 'I also found hair in my shower which matched the colour of the woman on one of his videos. The phone bills, however, were the last straw. He was calling her about a hundred times a month, and sending videos and pictures. We had a huge row and he told me I was crazy.'

The disadvantages of seeking evidence is that you never know what you will find or how you will feel. Although it might seem a relief to know the truth, realising that you are holding a love letter or finding a picture of the two of them together could feel very different indeed. Many people report feeling dizzy, sick and that their mind starts racing. When tackling their partner, they are more likely to be angry, combative and, ultimately, less likely to have a productive discussion. This is because the unfaithful partner will focus on calming down the Discoverer and underplay the seriousness of the affair.

However, turning detective can be empowering. 'I checked his computer history and temporary Internet files to find out what sites he had been frequenting. This shocked the life out of my husband as he always thought I was a complete technophobe,' says Carol, fifty-three.

Hearing it from other people

Although people who are unfaithful think nobody knows about their affair, it is generally obvious to their work colleagues. The two lovers might choose out-of-the-way places for a secret rendez-vous, but the chances of their being spotted are high. In fact, it is often only a matter of time before someone drops a heavy hint or reveals the truth. Hannah, thirty-eight, discovered her husband of almost twenty years had been cheating when a stranger rang her doorbell: 'There was a tall man, in his early forties, and he wanted to come into my house. He was all on edge. He made me so uncomfortable, I was about to close the door when he said, "It's about your husband and my wife." Instinctively, I knew the rest. In a trance, I stepped back and let him in. He had found texts and all sorts of correspondence. He showed me everything. He was really angry – like it was my fault, that I should control my husband better. I couldn't get him out of the house quick enough. Afterwards, I just sat there and stared out the window.'

Finding out from someone else is embarrassing and humiliating, even if the bad news comes from a friend or a family member who does everything to lessen the blow. The deceived partner immediately worries about who else knows and feels stupid that he or she was the last to find out. In some cases, they take out their anger on the bearer of the bad news, and spoil a good friendship, or automatically leap to their partner's defence. If the teller has no solid evidence, or the information comes from an anonymous letter or phone call, the deceiving partner will sometimes claim that this person bears a grudge and dismiss everything as tittle-tattle. Whatever the exact circumstances, the deceived partner is left wondering who she or he can trust and who has kept back information.

Unfortunately, there are few advantages to finding out this way. Sometimes, if the news comes from the spouse of your partner's lover, the two of you can support each other and share information. However, it is always better to hear the truth from your partner's lips rather than third-hand and filtered through someone with a very particular take on the situation.

Hearing it from the third party

When an affair is well established and the third party begins to feel that they have 'rights', she or he can feel it is in their interest to 'out' the affair. Cecilia discovered her husband's infidelity when one of her friends began to behave particularly unpleasantly. 'We all went out for a charity event. I wasn't wearing my glasses and apparently she spent the entire evening across the table from my husband dropping enormous hints and at one point mouthed "I love you". She also ran off the menu of a very expensive restaurant in Paris which she'd taken him to on her expense account and put the bill in his jacket pocket for me to find the next morning.' Finding out in this manner is also hard to handle. The deceived partner can feel angry, despairing and afraid. Sometimes she or he can be so overwhelmed that they lash out and become violent. The main problem, however, is working out the reliability of the testimony of the third party who will always have their own interests at heart.

Sometimes, there is empathy between the deceived partner and the third party. After all, they have both been 'used' in some way by the deceiver. The deceived partner may be reassured that the other man or woman is not as attractive or clever or accomplished as they had imagined. Alternatively, the deceived partner may be perplexed and not understand why their partner is attracted to the third party. Worst of all, the third party can make the deceived partner feel dowdy and unlovable.

When is an affair not an affair?

Our culture used to have pretty clear rules about what constituted cheating, but changes in the workplace and greater acceptability in having friends of the opposite sex have blurred the line. So it is perfectly possible to discover intimate texts and emails from your partner to another woman or man and to be told that they are 'innocent' and that the suspected other person in the affair is nothing more than 'a good friend'. However, your gut instinct is on red-alert and all the signs point to deception. So when does someone cross the line into adultery and what exactly constitutes deception?

Mark and Carrie are in their thirties; he works in the city and she is a supply teacher. Their relationship came under pressure when he was investigated for some trading irregularities. 'Carrie was busy with the children and, although she was supportive, she lost interest in the twists in complicated procedure,' says Mark, thirty-five, 'so I started talking to a colleague – just to get it out of my system. I accept that it was often over a glass of wine – but there were things that just couldn't be said in the office.'

Carrie had becomes suspicious and investigated: 'One Saturday, when he was supposed to have been looking after the children, he'd spoken to her three times and never for less than twenty minutes. We haven't talked that much in years.'

Mark admitted that he had started discussing home as well as work problems – in particular, Carrie's lack of interest in sex – but saw nothing wrong with this: 'I thought she could give me a female perspective,' he explained. Although Mark was cleared by the investigators at work, Carrie was not so forgiving: 'He might not have "done anything", as he keeps telling me, but it feels like a betrayal.'

21

Instead of trying to understand what went wrong and to repair their relationship, Mark and Carrie were too busy arguing about whether he had had an affair or not. Fortunately, in counselling, Mark accepted that the friendship had got of hand and was undermining his relationship. Carrie accepted that Mark had stopped short of having sex with the other woman: 'I suppose I have to give him credit for that but it still feels like cheating to me.' To short-circuit pointless arguments, I use the term 'inappropriate friendship' to describe these intense and dangerous extra-marital relationships.

So what is the difference between a genuine friendship and an inappropriate one? The key test is the level of secrecy. True friendship is open to scrutiny and there is no need to 'edit' the number of times the friends meet and what they discuss. In contrast, an inappropriate friend is only mentioned in passing, if ever, to a partner. True friendship is based on a common interest or activity. An inappropriate friendship is based on the strength of feelings between the friends. Of course, we talk about our problems to friends. However, we also respect our partner's confidentiality and do not share details that would embarrass him or her. Inappropriate friendships ignore these boundaries and confidential information is exchanged to deepen the bond. It is especially dangerous if someone tells their 'friend' something that they cannot tell, or are unwilling to share with, their partner.

It is very easy for an inappropriate friendship to tip over into a full-blown affair. The 'friends' have long, clandestine phone calls and share flirty texts. Each person is 'flattered' by the extra attention and this relationship becomes increasingly significant to their day-to-day happiness. Before long, the 'friends' are indulging in heavy petting, and crossing the line into sexual relations is ultimately not such a big jump. Indeed, Mark admitted his friendship would probably have turned sexual if Carrie had not intercepted him. There is also an on-line version of inappropriate friends where two people chat about a shared interest but the communication quickly becomes very personal. Soon the friends are staying up late to 'work' on the computer and lying to their partner about the amount of time spent on-line.

The number of cases in my therapy office involving inappropriate friendship has risen dramatically. This is partly because men have finally accepted that talking about problems is beneficial, except most of their male friends are hopeless at listening. 'Normally, if something's bugging me, I'd talk to my wife, but this time she was the problem,' says David, a 42-year-old fireman. 'The lads at work would have laughed and I don't really get on with my sister.' A female work colleague seemed the natural solution but this backfired and David got embroiled in an inappropriate friendship.

The other reason for the increase in inappropriate friends is the trend towards less hierarchical and more informal workplaces. Alice, twenty-nine, had a good relationship with her boss who had become her mentor, helping her with promotion and the pitfalls of office politics: 'I knew that he found me attractive but as it helped me get on, what was the harm? Well, one day I was really down about something at home and he caught me at a weak moment; he asked about the problem and I ended up in his office telling him all about it – at length. I found myself relying on our little chats. Without knowing it at the time, I'd crossed a line.' Throw into this mixture the increased number of hours that we spend at work, the trend for people to have friends of both sexes, and the ubiquity of the Internet, and inappropriate friendships are almost inevitable.

So what should you do if you suspect or discover your partner's inappropriate friendship? While branding it an affair, as Carrie did with Mark, will tip a worrying problem into a full-blown crisis, ignoring or playing the friendship down is just as dangerous. 'My husband had all these texts that said things like "miss you" and "love your laugh" but as I had been sneaking behind his back to uncover this, I felt guilty and didn't say anything,' says Jo Ellen, twenty-eight. 'I dropped hints and hoped he would say something, but he didn't. Several months later, he announced that our marriage had serious problems and that he wanted to leave. All my accusations came tumbling out and he admitted he had been talking to this woman, nothing more, but that she had been instrumental in helping him make his mind up.' Jo Ellen was incensed that he had not talked to her so that they could have solved their problems together and possibly saved their marriage.

If your partner has had or is having an inappropriate friendship, but has stopped short of an affair, it is important to recognise this fact. Be thankful that she or he has not crossed the final line. However, inappropriate friendships are still serious and, just like a full-blown affair, point to a problem in your relationship that urgently needs to be addressed. More importantly, the feelings of betrayal are just as strong and you will need to go through the same seven-stage process to reach recovery.

Shock

The first reaction to discovering that your partner has been cheating is shock and disbelief. There are often strong and over-whelming physical symptoms, too. These can include palpitations, chest pains, difficulty breathing, a knot in the stomach, feeling sick and headaches. This is a normal response to trauma. Stress hormones, like adrenaline, have been released into the blood-stream to help you cope with the enormity of what has happened.

'It was like he'd dropped an atom bomb in my lap,' explains Kirsty, thirty-five, when her husband of ten years calmly walked into the living room, asked her to switch off the TV and confessed to his three-month affair with one of her friends. 'Up to that moment, I thought things were fine. Okay, life had been hectic – kids, jobs, money – but still it wasn't bad. How could he have done this to me?' Kirsty's sense of betrayal was so profound that she felt that she was choking on her feelings. She ran to the toilet, where she was physically sick. 'Afterwards, I washed my hands and tried to be calm, but how could life ever be the same again?'

Another common reaction is feeling completely detached, as if the news of infidelity has been delivered to someone else. When Ellie, whose partner had love bites, finally had her partner's affair confirmed by the other woman, she was on lunch break from work. 'I wandered around the town centre in a daze for about half an hour. My heart was racing and I could hardly breathe. I have no idea how I managed not to get hit by a car because I crossed a few roads without even looking around me.' Other common symptoms of shock include: problems sleeping, poor appetite, being easily startled and an inability to concentrate or remember important facts. It is not uncommon, therefore, to need to go over the same conversation again – once the first effects of shock have worn off.

In most cases, the heightened levels of shock will last for about forty-eight hours. However, it is common for reminders – like finding more evidence – to bring back the symptoms again, but hopefully not with the same intensity, and recovery is quicker. Unfortunately, there are some people for whom the shock lasts longer. Especially if there has been some previous trauma such as childhood sexual abuse, a severe car accident or another affair. If the palpitations, sickness and memory loss last longer than two days, this is known as Acute Stress Disorder and, if it lasts longer than a month, as Post-Traumatic Stress Disorder. If this sounds familiar, you should consult your doctor. However, it is important to emphasise that shock is a normal reaction – a cushion against a terrible discovery.

By contrast, some people find shock energising. The adrenaline and the primitive 'fight or flight' instinct kick in. Natasha, forty-seven, could not bear to have her husband near her and took 'flight': 'I pulled off my wedding ring and went for a twenty-kilometre walk to get out and be alone.' For other people, the reaction is 'fight'. When Karen – whose husband had supposedly been installing computers in Whitehall – finally admitted to herself that her husband had been unfaithful, she took control. 'I went upstairs, on a hunch, and opened the drawer on his side of the bed and found incriminating photos and a diary cataloguing his affair during a transatlantic sailing race. I then checked credit-card statements and mobile phone bills – something I had never done before. It was all there. I was devastated.' In this case, the shock had been positive and had blasted Karen out of her wilful blindness.

Why it feels like your world has been turned upside down

When people talk about discovering their partner's infidelity, they use very dramatic imagery. 'The bottom fell out of my world' or 'My life has never been the same since' or 'I felt like the character in the Road Runner cartoon that runs and then realises they are standing on a tiny strand of earth that collapses'. Despite the fact that our newspapers are full of unfaithful celebrities, that cheating is a staple of TV drama, and that we hear about the direct evidence of adultery from our work colleagues, friends and family, infidelity never loses its power to shock when it happens to *us*. This is because it undermines three beliefs that underpin our lives:

1. The world is benevolent. (Good things happen to good people.)
2. The world is meaningful. (There is a plan and things happen for a reason.)
3. I am worthy. (Therefore good things will happen to me.)

Although deep down we know the world is more complicated, we have neither the desire nor the time to look at the unsettling truth. Instead, we cruise along protected by our faith in these three beliefs. However, infidelity makes us stop and realise the ugly truth. Even though we are a good provider, parent or home-maker, this does not necessarily keep our partner faithful. The world can be cruel and bad things happen for no particular reason. And if our relationship is not safe, what about our job and what about our friends: will they betray us too?

On the one hand, it seems cruel to point out the full devastation of infidelity. Haven't you got enough on your plate already? But on the other hand, it is important to understand why it hurts so much and to ensure that you are not being too hard on yourself. I will return to these three beliefs at other points along the journey. However, rest assured, your faith will slowly return and although tempered by experience, it will be more realistic, more grounded and more enduring.

The aftermath of discovery

It might feel that your heart is about to break but take comfort; everything that was in the shadows is now heading out into the light. The alternative is very bleak, as the following response to my questionnaire about infidelity shows. Connie is now sixty-four and has been married for twenty-three years. 'I knew from the beginning about the affair. He would throw his dinner in the bin because he'd already eaten in restaurants with her. I also found receipts for jewellery that I never received.' She confronted both her husband and the other woman, but for some reason did not follow through. 'I told him if I found concrete proof I would immediately divorce him. If he had loved me, and didn't want to lose me, he would have dropped her, but instead he kept on seeing her for four years. I became ill with worry but it didn't bother him. All he thought about was seeing her.'

This strange limbo, where she *knew* but didn't officially know, continued because Connie did not feel that she had any alternative. She hoped that if she ignored the affair, her marriage would improve. She was partially right. The other woman did eventually end it and go back to her husband. However, even ten years on, Connie's marriage remains frozen. 'It's not the fact that he has had an affair that has shattered our marriage, but that he was willing to throw everything away. I am second best and this will always be to the day I die. Even now, there is no hope of our marriage working and no affection or sex between us at all.' Her final two responses to my questionnaire are perhaps the bleakest of all. What has helped recovery? 'Nothing.' What have you learnt about your relationship? 'That we should never have got together in the first place.' I cannot help but wonder what Connie's life would have been like if she had been braver all those years ago. It is impossible to believe that it could have been worse. So if you find your courage waning and wonder if it might be better to close your eyes, remember the alternative. Facing up to the shock of discovery might be painful but it is also the first step on the road to recovery.

The Discovered and shock

It is no surprise that the Discoverer of infidelity will be shocked. After all, they have been lied to and kept in the dark. However, despite knowing everything, the Discovered often goes into shock too when confronted about the affair. This is because, just like the Discoverer, the Discovered has been in denial about how serious the situation has become. 'I met her on a course and there was a spark, so we kept in touch,' explains Edward, fifty-one. 'It was really well contained. We would see each other about once every six weeks. It didn't really mean much. We weren't soul partners or anything, but we did grow quite close. She helped me feel that I was still attractive and not sliding silently into decrepitude. I told myself, this was something for me and didn't have any impact on my wife – who seemed to treat me as part of the furniture.' When his wife found out – and laid out all the evidence of his infidelity – he was shocked at how often he had met the third party and how much he had spent on her. 'It didn't seem possible, I could have sworn it was half those times and just a couple of meals, but all the credit-card statements said something different.' He had, in effect, been so effectively *minimising* the importance of the affair that he had even convinced himself.

There is a second deadly force at play when people have affairs: *compartmentalisation*. This term was coined by Karen Horney, a German psychologist who emigrated to America in the thirties, and became both dean and founder of the American Institute for Psychology. She was interested in how people dealt with contradictory thoughts, feelings, beliefs or roles. A classic example would be a fervent Roman Catholic who uses contraceptives or someone who believes in equality of opportunity but sends their child to a private school. To some extent, we all build walls to section off parts of our life. In this way, we can be ruthless at work and loving at home and tell ourselves: that's just the way it is. However, in compartmentalisation, these two worlds become watertight sealed boxes where the action in one world, supposedly, has no impact on the other. Therefore, someone who is unfaithful will say: 'It's just for me' or 'It helps me deal with stress' and not have to face the impact on their partner or family.

Julia, forty-two, filled in my questionnaire about infidelity. She has been married for twenty-one years and ten months ago started an affair with a man she knew when she was sixteen. 'My affair is very important to me and well contained,' she writes. 'I don't feel guilty but very happy and have a relatively happy marriage too. There are no problems because we are careful and cautious. We live sixty miles apart and sometimes cannot meet for two to three weeks. However, I feel more valued, loved, sexual and, instead of feeling like a wife and mother, feel more like an individual.' In answer to the question about her greatest regret, she replied: 'I don't have any as yet. It is all under control and both situations are manageable.' This attitude is only possible because she has compartmentalised both halves of her life.

However, life is seldom so neat and, over time, the walls crumble between the two worlds. David is a forty-year-old academic, who met his mistress at a conference: 'At the time, it didn't seem like betraying my wife. It was a bit like: "What happens at conference, stays at conference". My lover had a keen mind and helped me sharpen my thought process and get my work into some important publications. It was good for my career.' At the same time, David saw himself as a conscientious husband and father. He worked hard, brought in a good salary and tried to make himself available to ferry his teenage children around. He saw no contradiction between his two lives because each was barricaded off from the other.

However, it is impossible to stop one life leaking into another and David started to see his mistress more frequently. He also became moody and distracted: 'I would pick fights with my wife over the smallest of things and somehow the fact that we weren't getting on justified me seeing another woman.' When his wife discovered the affair – he had left condoms in the glove pocket of his car – he was shocked by the depth of her feelings: 'She was angry, hurt, betrayed. She blamed herself. She cried and cried and cried. I couldn't believe it. I'd convinced myself that she didn't really care.' His carefully constructed compartments came tumbling down. 'The children were really upset and worried but I'd never thought of the impact on them.'

When I counselled David, he was considering what to do next. He and his mistress had fantasised about starting a new life together and he talked about making this a reality: 'The children will cope, it's not like it's that unusual these days,' he explained. This is the third kind of defence against reality: *rationalisation.*

Using this strategy, it is possible to overlook the emotional impact of infidelity. 'Schools are set up to cope with this sort of thing. There are counsellors and the children have friends who have been through something similar,' David explained to me. Being rational, he is correct. Schools are better set up to help with the emotional fall-out and some of the stigma has been removed. However, when David stopped treating his children as a group and instead looked at their individual personalities, it became clear that divorce would not be so straightforward. 'My youngest has become very clinging,' he admitted. So I asked about his mistress's children: how did he think he would get on with them? He looked at me, stunned. 'I've never thought about that.' In affair world, they could be airbrushed out of the picture. In the real world, he faced life with two angry and disruptive teenage stepchildren. Compartmentalisation had kept the two worlds firmly apart.

So when the compartmentalised walls crumble, the full impact of the infidelity is laid bare and all the rationalisation is blown away; many deceivers go into shock and, just like the deceived, are unable to think straight. They feel sick and horrified by the enormity of what they have done. Graham is forty-three and had an affair with a work colleague for eighteen months but his wife found papers, correspondence and emails. 'I had never felt anything like it before,' he says about being discovered. 'I was in a total state of shock. I thought I'd woken from a nightmare

– except I hadn't woken. The reality of what I'd done, being faced with all the facts, it was horrendous and went against everything I thought I'd believed in. I had let down my wife, betrayed her trust so utterly. And at a secondary level, too, I had lied to friends, relations, anyone who could have helped me. I had so much explaining to do at work, at home, in every walk of my life. I had no idea where to start, or who to turn to. I wanted help badly but felt that there was none.' There will be more from Graham later in this book, but his story underlines how shock is not just reserved for the deceived.

For the Discovered: Shock and Disbelief

- If you are confused about what you want and how to move forward, this book will provide clarity and a path to heal your primary relationship and ultimately to restore trust again.

- How did you get into this dilemma? Unfortunately, the less you put into your relationship, the less you will get out of it. Conversely, the more energy you put into it, the better it will be. (This is backed up by research at Tel Aviv University that shows people are three times more likely to perform well when others have high expectations of them.)

  By the end of my seven-step programme, you will emerge with a stronger and more loving relationship – but only if you take action and start investing time and energy again.

- It is better to tell your partner about your infidelity than to consciously or unconsciously leave clues lying around to be discovered. This strategy hands over to the person least well-equipped to deal with the fall-out of an affair the responsibility of making the first move.

- If you put off telling your partner, the likelihood of someone else telling them – like a work colleague, friend, family member, or even your lover – will increase.

- If your partner challenges you and asks about your infidelity, your instinct may be to deny it but this will only add to your partner's humiliation, the damage to your relationship, and the pain for everyone concerned when the affair is finally uncovered.

- When making a confession about infidelity, keep to the main facts and be guided by your partner as to how much detail she or he wants to hear.

- It is important to make honesty your new policy. Do not try and soften the blow by hiding unpleasant details. They will come out eventually. Remember, politicians are brought down not by the original sin but by the cover-up. Conversely, those who confess before the public find out are often forgiven.

- Unless you are truthful about the full extent of your feelings for the third party, your partner will have no idea as to the extent of work needed to either repair your relationship or to separate less painfully.

- Once someone knows the worst, it is amazing how quickly they can gather up their strength and cope. What is much harder is uncertainty, continued deception and never knowing where one stands.

- Sometimes unfaithful partners, who come alone to an initial pre-counselling session, ask if they need to confess. Wouldn't it be kinder to keep the affair quiet and just tackle the underlying unhappiness?

  However, a secret is a major handicap to healing. In a 2005 study, reported in the Journal of Consulting and Clinical Psychology, 134 couples were recruited for marital therapy. They were studied before counselling, at thirteen weeks, twenty-six weeks and after their final session. The secret infidelity couples – where the affair remained unacknowledged – were significantly more distrustful of each other than the ones with acknowledged infidelity (and the couples who were tackling issues other than infidelity). Their distress had been relieved slightly at thirteen weeks but after that the situation rapidly deteriorated. Ultimately, all the secret infidelity cases were treatment failures.

- Remember lies got you into this hole; truth is the only way out.

New skill: Open your mind

With each step on the road from discovery to recovery, you will learn a new skill. These skills will not only help with the fall-out from infidelity but also with life in general. The first is 'Open your mind'. To an extent, you have already started by facing up to your suspicions and discovering the truth. However, there is a harder component. Unfortunately, human beings do not like to deal with conflicting thoughts and beliefs. How can our partner claim to love us but still cheat on us? How can he or she be unfaithful and a good parent? These things are logically incompatible and it makes us anxious and uncomfortable.

Psychologists call this *cognitive dissonance*. It was named by an American Social psychologist called Leon Festinger. In the fifties, he studied a UFO doomsday cult lead by a Chicago housewife who claimed that the city was about to be flooded. When the prophecy failed, he expected the followers to abandon their leader. However, they increased their proselytising: while previously they had shunned media interest, they started giving interviews about how their faith had saved the city. This is a good example of cognitive dissonance, because the followers ignored any evidence that contradicted their beliefs and instead looked for evidence to reinforce them.

Applying these ideas to infidelity, we find it hard to cope with the possibility that our partner can be simultaneously a good and a bad person. Our natural tendency is to plump for just one picture – in this case, the bad one. However, if you give into cognitive dissonance, you will notice only evidence of your partner's badness and downplay any evidence of his or her goodness. (This is why some people cast their partner as a bad parent too and stop the children from seeing them.)

It is the same process with responsibility for the affair, which is all loaded on to one partner. In fact, in popular parlance, we talk about the *guilty* party and the *innocent* party. However, in twenty-five years of counselling couples, I have yet to meet any couple where the divisions were this black and white. Having said that, the couples who thought in these terms found it hardest to recover. This is why the new skill of opening your mind is so important. In this way, you will be able to hold on to all the competing information about your partner – without rushing too soon to judgement. It will be tough but, as you will discover, it will pay dividends.

Summary
- If your instincts make you suspect your partner's fidelity, take stock. How trustworthy have these instincts been in the past?
- It is better to confront your partner calmly, and give her or him the opportunity to confess, than to search for evidence.
- An inappropriate friendship or an online affair is still damaging to a relationship, even if there has been no sexual infidelity, and should not be ignored.
- It is natural for both the Discoverer and the Discovered to feel shock.
- It is hard to reconcile the picture, built up over many years together, of a loving partner, mother or father with the person who has lied, cheated, and threatens everyone's happiness.
- However, by learning to deal with cognitive dissonance, you can hold both your own vision of the relationship and your partner's at the same time – and accept that they will not always be the same thing. This will be invaluable not just through the rest of the seven steps but through your life together.

Exercises

Improve your communication style

Here are six ways of getting on better on a day-to-day basis, bringing issues out into the open and stopping rows from escalating needlessly.

1. *Lower the general temperature*

One of the key factors determining whether a couple will thrive is the ratio between positive strokes (compliments, saying thank you, paying attention, doing nice things for each other) and negative strokes (complaints, criticism, ignoring, doing spiteful things). We like to think that one positive stroke will cancel out one negative one. However, researchers at the University of Washington in Seattle discovered that it takes five positives to remove one negative. From my own marital therapy practice, I find that couples who claim that they cannot communicate are actually communicating – but only with negative strokes.

- Monitor yourself for twenty-four hours: How many times do you compliment, say thank you or go the extra mile for your partner? How often do you complain, criticise or get snappy?
- Could you increase the number of positive strokes?
- I am not suggesting that you make up compliments or do anything false. Instead, look at the internal dialogue that's going on in your head. You may think: 'that's a nice dress' or 'it was a real help picking the children up from school' but these thoughts often remain unexpressed and private. Instead, say these things out loud and let your partner know.

2. *Improve your body language*

General stress and lack of time means that we often try and communicate with our partner by shouting up the stairs or when they are watching TV, reading the paper, or working on the computer.

- Make the commitment to be in the same room when you have something to ask or tell. Even if it is something minor like: 'What time are you coming home?' This will minimise any misunderstandings.
- Look at your partner when you speak or when she or he is talking, turn down the TV, put down the paper or turn away from the computer screen.
- Maintain eye contact.
- Nod your head from time to time as this will encourage your partner to tell you more.
- Do not fold your arms as this can appear defensive.

3. *Check how you talk to your partner*
For many couples, the problem is not what they say but how they say it. So start with less stressful situations like work, friends or family members and then incorporate these lessons when communicating with your partner.

- Use 'I' rather than 'you'. For example: 'I am angry' – nobody can argue with that, you are the expert on your feelings. By contrast, 'You make me angry' will instantly get your partner defensive or ready to attack.
- For couples whose arguments quickly escalate, I ban them from saying 'you' altogether for five minutes. Try it and see what difference it makes.
- Own your opinions rather than make general statements. For example: 'In my opinion, the kitchen shouldn't be left like that.' You can even back it up with an explanation – 'I can't bear the mess' or 'it's unhygienic'. This invites a debate and a possible solution. By contrast, a general statement like 'Dirty plates shouldn't be left on the counter' sounds like a proclamation from an all-powerful emperor and invites rebellion.
- Do not bring in the opinions of other people. This will only escalate a debate into a row. It does not matter what your friends, your mother or every right-thinking person

does. It's your house and your relationship and it's what the two of you think that counts.

4. *Show respect for each other's opinions*
Respect is one of the most powerful ways of giving your partner positive strokes. Conversely, losing respect for each other seriously undermines a relationship.

- Listen to what your partner has to say without interrupting.
- Do not use the time that he or she is speaking to rehearse your own point of view.
- Show that you have really listened, and digested what your partner has said, by repeating key phrases: 'You planned to clear the garage first' or 'So you were already late'.
- Give positive feedback: 'That's a good point' or 'I agree with that'.
- Seek clarification, and check that you have heard right: 'So what you're saying is that you're angry that I didn't put my plate in the dishwasher'. If you're wrong, your partner will soon correct you: 'Not angry, just frustrated.'

5. *Deal with things as they come up*
When couples are under stress, they try and remove all the negative strokes and avoid making any complaints. However, it is impossible for two people to live together without some disagreement. So accept that there will be differences and have a strategy for solving them.

- It is always easier to tackle one problem at a time, rather than let a whole pile of issues build up and row about them all.
- Saying something at the time allows your partner to act. (For example, by saying 'Please could you pick me up from the station', you are giving your partner the chance to oblige. By contrast, saying nothing sets up a future row: 'And you couldn't even be bothered to collect me from the station on

Friday night.' On Saturday morning, this is history and too late for your partner to do anything about it.)

- Make certain that you complain about a specific piece of behaviour ('Don't leave your wet towels on the bathroom floor') rather than criticise your partner's personality ('You're lazy and thoughtless').

6. *Don't let a row hang in the air*

Arguments can be very productive. They get feelings out into the open. They sort the important from the trivial. They clear the air. However, arguments are not productive when they involve days of stand-off, silence and a poisonous atmosphere.

- When enough time has passed to cool down, do a post-mortem on the argument. Where did it become unmanageable? How could you have done things differently?
- Apologise for your part in the breakdown: 'I'm sorry that I lost my temper' or 'I didn't mean to criticise'.
- Explain the background. Sometimes there is an extra piece of information that your partner needs: 'I had a really bad day at work and so was really grumpy and overreacted' or 'My mother would complain about just the same thing to my father'.
- Look for a compromise. What could both of you do differently? Could you trade? For example: 'I'll do ....
if you do ....'.
- Solutions that stick have a benefit for both sides. So look for something where everybody wins.

How to reprogram the unnaturally suspicious mind

There are two types of suspicions: 'natural' and 'unnatural'. The first is based on sound evidence of repeated strange or unusual behaviour over a period of time. (It normally turns out that your partner has been cheating.) The second is based on one small incident, which other people would probably not register, but because you are hyper-alert or tired or stressed, your imagination builds and builds until you decide that your partner *must* be cheating. (However, when you have calmed down, there is always a reasonable answer and the sensible part of your personality knows it is a false alarm.) If your suspicions fall into the first category, this exercise is not for you. Instead, you should confront your partner. If your suspicions fall into the second category, you have probably confronted your partner ten million times before. He or she has become so exasperated with being accused of cheating – even though he or she is patently not – that your whole relationship is in jeopardy. This exercise is for you:

1. *Take stock.* How often have you been sure that your partner has been unfaithful, or feared that the relationship is over, in the past three months? Comparing the frequency of your explosions with the same time last year, do they happen more frequently? How does your partner feel? Is this need to quiz, check up on and confront seriously undermining your relationship? Instead of beating yourself up and worrying that you are driving your partner away – which just throws fuel on the fire – make a commitment to change.

2. *What's in it for you.* At first sight, the answer would seem to be not much. However, deep down there is a reward – or you wouldn't keep doing it. So let's look at the pattern and try and discover the unconscious drivers: You have had a bad day. You are stressed and feel unloved. You need a cuddle and to be told that you are fabulous. (However, it is hard to ask outright – as you might be turned down and that would be worse than not asking.) Your partner does not instantly pick up on your need – perhaps she or he has had a tough day too – and you begin to worry that your partner does not love you. You need a guarantee. You check up. You pick a fight or needle him or her until you get a reaction (probably

it's negative attention but it's better than nothing). Ultimately, the two of you will make up and you will get the 'proof' that your partner cares. Most naturally suspicious people are just looking for reassurance, love and attention. However, the way that they go about getting it just drives people away.

3. *Be more realistic.* Most naturally suspicious people have sky-high expectations. They will not just get married and be happy ever after but will live in a thatched cottage with a white picket fence. They will always wear designer labels, there will never be baby sick on their clothes, and they will win salesperson of the month – every month. These are perfectionists and even one step off the primrose path equals complete failure and being unlovable. Unfortunately, however hard perfectionists try, life is never like this. There are times when demands at work prevent their partner from phoning five times a day or always taking their call. However, if naturally suspicious people cut themselves – and those they love – a little slack, life would be a whole lot easier. Okay, it might only be a 'normal' life but reality is ultimately always more satisfying than fantasy.

4. *Divert.* Understanding the patterns is only half the battle for changing the naturally suspicious mind. When you are under stress, you will also need first aid. If your mind starts racing, put up a mental STOP sign and do something nice: make yourself a cup of tea, read an inspiring book, take a bath or meditate. Diverting is particularly important if an overactive brain stops you from sleeping. Middle-of-the-night analysing rarely provides any useful insights and just feeds anxiety and fear. So get up and do something which occupies your brain but which is not too engrossing – like a jigsaw or a sudoku puzzle.

5. *Learn to calm yourself down.* When you are feeling good about your relationship and your partner is loving and attentive, it is easy to listen to the sensible voice in your head. So while your sensible voice is in charge, write down all the positive things about your relationship. For example: 'He really loves me' or 'She must care or she wouldn't put up with this'. And 'He's nothing like my last boyfriend who cheated' or 'She's nothing like my mother'. Find as many positive statements as you can and transfer them on to cards. Next time you find your suspicious voice getting the upper hand, bring out the cards and take a reality check. Tell yourself to STOP. Then allow your sensible voice to calm down your suspicious one. With a little practice, you will soon learn to soothe yourself rather than rely on your partner.

My lifeline
This exercise is designed to help you to understand your life up to this point and to begin to put what has just happened into a larger context. It can be done by both the Discoverer and the Discovered.

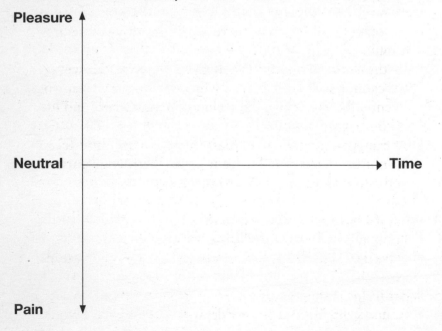

Copy the graph opposite and plot the highs and lows from your childhood to today. Then mark on the graph what was happening at these significant moments.

How to use and interpret your lifeline
  1. Look back at your previous low points.
     • What helped you climb out?
     • How could you harness those skills again?
     • What did you learn from the bad times?

  2. Look back at the high points.
     • What helped sustain them?
     • What did you learn from the good times? (Don't worry if there are fewer lessons under this heading. As you will discover, adversity is always the best teacher.)

  3. What about the flat lines?
     • These occur when people have done their best to ignore or suppress unpleasant or unwelcome feelings. They tell themselves: 'It doesn't matter', that they should 'turn the other cheek' or that 'there are bigger things to worry about'.
     • In the short term, this strategy will work. However, we cannot pick and choose which feelings we turn off. Eventually, even the good feelings are turned off and life becomes grey.
     • The anger of an affair can blast through a flat-line life, so do not be afraid to embrace it, argue with your partner and allow all the passions to surface.

  4. What if I have a lot of ups and downs?
     • Look at what has caused these swings.
     • Have they been due to bad luck or is there a bigger pattern?

  5. What if this is the lowest low?
     • At first sight, this can be very depressing. However, I would

ask you to consider if you have been 'over' dramatic. Do you wish to change your lifeline at all?

- If your partner's adultery is truly the worst event in your life to date, imagine that you can travel back to the earliest low in your life. Perhaps it was the first time that you had your heart broken by a boy or a girl.
- Imagine that the person that you are today can talk to this younger version of yourself. What comfort can you offer? What advice can you give?
- Now use this same advice and comfort to start digging yourself out of today's low.

Checkpoint

Three key points for surviving Stage One: Shock and Disbelief

1. Ask your partner rather than accuse him or her of having an affair.
2. Be calm when laying out your concerns, so your partner is less likely to turn defensive or aggressive.
3. Avoid using absolute terms like 'never', 'always' and 'should' when discussing problems, as these provoke a row rather than a debate.

Stage Two:
Intense Questioning

RECOVERY

Intense Questioning

Shock and Disbelief

DISCOVERY

When the shock begins to wear off, the Discoverer of infidelity is flooded with a million and one questions. Who is the other woman or man? How long has it been going on? How many people know? Does this mean the relationship is over? Emergency medical teams or detectives investigating a missing person or crime scene talk about the golden hour – when the opportunity for saving the patient or solving the crime is at its height. There is a golden window for rescuing a relationship from the adultery trap too. Rest assured, it is more than sixty minutes. The infidelity golden period lasts for about six months. So don't panic or go rushing off in several directions at the same time, telling everybody, complicating matters and possibly trampling over important evidence.

The need to understand

Once the bare facts of the infidelity have been assimilated – who, how long, what happened – the Discoverer needs to make sense of everything. This is why I call Stage Two: Intense Questioning. As Marie, forty-five, explained: 'Once I know the truth, and I've processed it, I know I can cope. What I can't deal with is not knowing.' However, there is so much to discover that you can easily be overwhelmed and, with no idea what to expect, frightened too. Therefore, it is important to chop problems down into manageable chunks and to focus on the main job of this stage – finding out as much as possible about the affair – and leave processing this information until later. Here are five strategies for getting the most out of your golden window:

Improve your interview techniques

The first in-depth discussions about the affair are particularly important and should not be hurried.

- Keep the questions open. For example: 'When did you first meet her or him?' rather than 'Did it start six months ago?', which might lead your partner to give an answer that he or she thinks you want.

- Don't rush into making a judgement. You might want to call the third party a 'tart' or a 'bastard' but this will make your partner clam up, become defensive or start defending their lover. This is a blind alley and will not help your overall understanding.

- Discover the overall state of mind of your partner at the moment when the affair started: 'What was going on in your life at this point?' 'How did you feel?' This is the first clue to why he or she was unfaithful.

- The best way to understand is to piece together the story of the infidelity. Right from the beginning of time, mankind has told stories in order to make sense of the world. Slowly lead your partner through the events: 'What happened next?' or 'And then what?'

- Stories have a beginning, a middle and an end. Do not be tempted to skip ahead to something that makes you particularly anxious as this will only confuse and make it harder to see the full picture.

- Try and keep calm. The more upset or accusatory you become, the more your partner will try and appease you. This can involve skipping unpleasant but important pieces of information (for example, he introduced his lover to his mother after they bumped into her while out shopping together), downplaying how she or he feels about the third party, or, worse still, telling out-right lies.

- Get clarification. A lot of the information will not make sense, partly because you are in shock and partly because you probably thought your relationship was perfectly adequate –

48

at least on the surface. So repeat back important sentences as this will prompt your partner to expand and explain.

- Don't assume. Although the intention behind some of your partner's actions might seem clear, don't jump to conclusions but ask instead. For example: 'Did you mean to punish me?' or 'Did you want to hurt me?' It is probable that your partner will have a different take.
- Silence is a particularly useful tool for gathering information. So do not leap in with the next question, just nod your head or sit quietly. This is often the moment when crucial details are revealed.
- Do not expect to cover everything in one go. In the next few days, you will probably have more questions and at this stage most unfaithful partners are happy to try and explain their behaviour.

Learn to spot evasions and equivocation

In my survey into adultery in the UK, 62 per cent of Discoverers reported that their partners held back important information about the infidelity. 'He told me that he only had sex with her once,' explains Ellie whom we met in the first chapter. 'However, about three months later, he slipped up and said it was ten or fifteen times. I still think that is a gross underestimate.'

Sometimes, people lie to cover smaller but still hurtful details: 'I could live with the physical side of the relationship,' says Sybil, thirty-three, 'but I found later, when he'd forgotten that he lied, that he had spent some Sundays with her and her friends when he claimed to be with his mates. He also took her on holiday when he said he needed some space to think.'

At this stage, it is hard to know when your partner is telling the truth – after all, he or she has consistently lied while conducting the affair. So here are some tell-tale signs that point to evasion or equivocation:

- Playing for time: asking 'Can you repeat the question?' or pretending not to have heard. This is because liars need to think up a plausible answer or make certain their lies do not contradict each other.

- Asking for definitions: 'What do you mean by unfaithful?' This technique is a variation of playing for time but is principally aimed at reducing the scope of a question.
- Preambles to the answer which are a little bit too reassuring. 'The truth is . . .' or 'I don't want you to think I'm blowing you off . . .' These are smokescreens designed to make a lie seem more credible.
- Sarcasm and humour. 'You would say that . . .' This tactic is used to put the questioner on the back foot and become defensive.
- Providing a juicy titbit of information to distract your attention. Instead of answering the question, your partner throws you off the scent.
- Something about the explanation does not add up.

Encourage truthfulness

After being discovered, only a few people go on lying in order to *continue* their affair (in my survey, it was only 8 per cent). The majority have more complex motives: they fear the whole truth will destroy their relationship, they want to protect their own backs, they are too ashamed to face-up to the full extent of their betrayal, or they wish to avoid further hurting their partner. Whatever the motive, or combination of motives, it drives the Discoverer almost to the point of madness and prolongs this intense questioning phase. Here are some strategies to help you to move forward:

- Build a rapport with your partner. The following phrases reduce confrontation and encourage honesty: 'I know you wish we weren't having this conversation' or 'This is painful for both of us.'
- Locate the blockages. Ask your partner what is holding him or her back. Try prompts such as: 'You think that I will be upset and we'll fight' (suggests fear), or 'You may be thinking I'm making a bigger thing out of this' (suggests

shame) or 'I know you don't want to hurt my feelings' (suggests protection).

- Give your partner an update on your feelings. He or she will probably expect the worst, but it is probable that you have absorbed and begun to deal with some aspects of the infidelity. For example: 'I understand that you felt neglected but I don't understand . . .' or 'I can accept that you were tempted and had sex but not that . . .' Stating aloud your private thoughts will not only clarify the situation for you but also provide a breakthrough for your partner.
- Explain why honesty is so important. For example: 'I'd rather hear it from you first', 'I can live with what happened but not with your lying', 'It will clear the air', 'Getting this off your chest will make you feel better' or 'It will save a lot of heartache and we can begin to put this behind us.'
- Ask yourself if your partner has justifiable fears about a full confession. Will you immediately order him or her out of the house? Will you throw things or become aggressive or even violent? Will you take out your anger on the third party? Will you use the information to turn the children against your partner? Will you rush to judgement and not hear the whole story?
- Monitor your reaction to new nuggets of information. Be careful not to seize on them as opportunities to vent your anger. (Although this is very tempting, and possibly justifiable, it will make your partner clam up and provide a justification for future silences.) Conversely, proving your partner's fears of an explosion to be groundless will turn a trickle of information into a flood.

Do you really need to know everything?

On the one hand, it is necessary to have a full picture of the infidelity so that you can make an informed choice about whether or not to fight for the relationship. On the other hand, there comes a time when further digging is counterproductive and makes the Discovered despair. So what is the correct balance?

'I really needed the gory details,' says Jessica, twenty-eight, who had been living with her partner for five years. 'I wanted to know if she was better in bed. Did she have a better technique and, if so, what was it? What did she look like? Was she prettier? Were her breasts firmer? I went on and on, until finally he told me everything.' Jessica thought this knowledge would help her 'move on' but it had the opposite effect: 'It was like she was always in the bed with us.' The couple split up a few weeks later.

Graham, forty-three, whom we met in the first chapter, found his partner's need-to-know relentless: 'Although I told her pretty much everything, I just wanted to forget. But she kept wanting all the fine detail, of where we had stayed, where we had sex, what sex we had had, the email accounts with which I had communicated, the emails themselves, the text messages, the poetry I sent her. It was awful bringing it all back up and I'm still not sure it helped particularly.'

Every Discoverer will want to know different amounts and different sorts of information. There is no right or wrong position. To help you find the right balance for yourself and your relationship, ask the following questions:

- Am I trying to punish my partner by making him or her go over the same information again and again?
- Am I punishing myself for not being attentive enough in the past or because of some other perceived failing?
- Am I making my partner repeat details in the hope of catching her or him out and discovering something new? If so, how productive is this strategy?
- Am I in danger of getting stuck in the Intense Questioning stage?
- Is my behaviour making a drama out of a crisis?
- What would help me move on to the next stage?
- How could I calmly explain my needs to my partner?
- When would be a good time to do this?

The role of sex in infidelity

An affair always puts the spotlight on a couple's sex life. This is painful enough but, worse still, it can also reveal two fundamentally different attitudes. These are best summed up by movie legend Mae West: 'Sex with love is the greatest thing in life. But sex without love – that's not so bad either.' For some people, sex equals love. For others, sex equals sex plus sometimes love too. Traditionally, the first has been seen as a female perspective and the latter as a male but, as Mae West (1893–1980) shows, it has never been this clear cut. If couples ever talk about love and sex, they will generally agree that sex without love is empty and meaningless – anything else would lead to a fight, unhappiness and possibly even divorce. So whatever our past experiences and our private personal thoughts, we smile and agree. Unfortunately, an affair blows this cosy conspiracy out of the water.

When Samantha, thirty-five, found that Mark, thirty-nine, had been having an affair with one of her friends, she was naturally devastated: 'I would never have sex with someone unless I truly loved them. I would never even think about sleeping with someone unless I was seriously contemplating spending the rest of my life with him. So it would probably be a clear signal that my marriage was well and truly over.' So, naturally, her first question – when she found a present from the other woman in the car – was: 'Do you love her?' Mark's reaction was typical: 'Of course not, I love you. It meant nothing.' Mark and Samantha are not alone in discovering that sex meant something different to each of them.

Researchers at the University of North Carolina looked at what felt like a greater betrayal: sexual or emotional infidelity. They discovered that men are more upset by sexual betrayal (73 per cent) than emotional (27 per cent). In contrast, women were more concerned by emotional betrayal (68 per cent) than sexual (32 per cent). This partially explains why men are more likely to keep back details about sex (frequency, where, what they enjoyed) while woman are more likely to hold back about their feelings (how much she loved and the depth of her emotions).

Researchers at Indiana State University were interested in whether gender differences were simply genetic or whether sexuality played a part, so they surveyed both heterosexuals and homosexuals but this time did not force a choice between either sexual or emotional betrayal. Heterosexual men still came out as the most jealous, not only topping the poll for being concerned about sexual infidelity but emotional infidelity also. (This is down to what the researchers call 'double-shot' fears. In other words, heterosexual men believed that if a woman was emotionally unfaithful she would probably be sexually unfaithful too.) The results for emotional infidelity were: heterosexual men 55 per cent, heterosexual women 30 per cent, gay men 24 per cent, lesbian women 22 per cent. The results for sexual infidelity were: heterosexual men 29 per cent, heterosexual women 11 per cent, gay men 5 per cent and lesbian women 4 per cent.

The issues around sexual infidelity are further complicated by the ubiquity of pornography as many people discover that their partner has been visiting adult chat rooms or watching X-rated movies. Every couple has to decide for themselves what constitutes betrayal and the border between acceptable and unacceptable behaviour. However, these discussions can further increase the sense that a partner has become a stranger and make recovery harder. (There is more on 'How to talk about sex' in the exercise section.)

What about the third party?

If it is hard to establish the full extent of the infidelity and the importance of sex, it is even harder to gauge the Discovered's true feelings towards the third party. There are two reasons for this. First, being found out bursts the private bubble of an affair and radically changes everyone's feelings. (Therefore, your partner will probably be confused or not know how she or he feels towards the third party.) Second, it is impossible to predict the reaction of the third party, whether he or she will retreat or fight for the relationship and what impact this decision will have on your partner. Whatever the circumstances, there will be an overriding need to know: Does he love her? Does she love him? And is it over?

Your partner and the third party

Modern technology means that much of the communication between your partner and the third party will have been saved. If you have read texts and emails (something I would not recommend), there will be a lot of hurtful things that will stick in your memory. 'He said she was his "soul mate" and "understood him better than anyone else" and that "their love will last for ever and ever",' said Laurie, thirty-eight. 'What I can't reconcile is that he now says it was not really serious and he doesn't really have any feelings for her.' To understand the stark differences between what her partner says and what he wrote, it is important to understand the role of fantasy in affairs.

Real relationships are built on small acts of service ('He will drop her off at the station' or 'She will shop for his mum when she comes out of hospital') and long stretches of time getting to really know each other. In stark contrast, the secrecy of an affair means that these everyday exchanges are absent, and fantasy – however implausible – rushes in to fill the gap. In many affairs, fantasy is all the lovers have and it gets pumped up to the epic statements that Laurie discovered. The reality is often rather banal. So if you find damning love letters, treat them as an insight into the relationship at the moment they were written but not the gospel truth about your partner's feelings today.

Dealing with the third party

The problems of unravelling real emotions from those pumped-up by fantasy are highlighted by Isabella whose husband of sixteen years had an affair: 'He promised that it was over but said that he needed some space.' They separated and went into counselling. Throughout this time, she found it hard to understand her husband's feelings: 'Sometimes he would be distant, or tearful, and a couple of times promised me that his affair was over. He said we were still working to get back together and on no account were we to see other people. Sometimes I got suspicious and asked if he was seeing her again. After all, we were living apart and what was to stop him? He thought it sounded like I was trying to push him into her arms. He vehemently denied seeing her again, would get quite angry and said he was having a nervous breakdown.' During this time, they started dating again and eventually, after four months, he asked to move back into the family house.

For the first six weeks after he returned, everything was fine. 'Then his lover phoned me with the "you have the right to know" speech. They had carried on the affair until he came home. She begged me to let her have him, as she had left her own husband for him. For about three days, she pestered me with calls and texts. She came to our house, when I was out, and our young children had to see my husband and her arguing outside. She stormed off, he rang her to see if she was okay, so she threatened suicide. He got a neighbour in for the children and sped off after her. The next day he finished it again, but that evening she called again and threatened to come over.'

Unfortunately, it gets worse. 'I called her, lost it and screamed at her. My husband called me a bitch. Then he told me I should've let him finish it the way he wanted. So he phoned her back again and sat apologising to her for half an hour.'

This might sound extreme but I have also counselled a man whose mistress tried three separate times to kill herself – fortunately she did not succeed. So what should you do if the third party has become a nuisance?

Graham, whom we met earlier, rang his mistress on the morning that the affair was out in the open: 'I told her that it was over and she said that she understood. She then tried to contact me by telephone, text message and email for the next three to four months. I set up blocks on my email account but she changed her email address. I got a digital telephone for home that could block numbers and she rang from different numbers. She only stopped when our solicitor wrote a letter threatening an injunction.' This practical approach will work much better than direct confrontation.

Common pitfalls in the first days and weeks after discovery

With all the stress and high-intensity feelings at this stage, everyone does something or says something that they later regret. So don't be too worried if you recognise any of the following traps:

Reacting first and thinking second

When Tracey, forty-five, discovered that her husband, Paul, had been both sexually and emotionally unfaithful, whereas previously he'd sworn it was just an inappropriate friendship, she erupted. 'The anger was so explosive that I started chucking things at him: the ashtray, a glass of wine, the rest of our supper. He was covered in ash and glass and stains and still I couldn't bear the sight of him. I ordered him out of the house but he refused until I threatened that I'd phone my son [from her first marriage] who's a big lad.' Finally, late at night, Paul fled. Not only is violence unacceptable, but Tracey had not thought through where he would go.

Paul takes up the story: 'I was having trouble checking into the local Travelodge, because I looked a right state and had given a different name to the one on my credit card. Where could I go? I literally had nowhere.' At this point, he had had no contact with the other woman for over two months. 'I thought it was all over between me and my wife – she had told me as much and in no uncertain terms – so I phoned her [the third party]'. The woman invited Paul over and, unsurprisingly, they ended up in bed together.

Fortunately, the affair did not reignite and after a couple of days Paul confessed what happened. Paul and Tracey were finally able to work through the blockage which had been caused by him being dishonest and the setback caused by her explosion.

Tip: If you are prone to acting first and thinking second, build in some 'time out'. This could be as little as half an hour or as long as twelve hours. Next time you feel the anger building up, step away and do something else. For example, make a cup of tea, take the dog for a walk or go for a run. When you have calmed down a little, take another look at the situation and talk to your partner. If your partner tries to intervene or pacify you during 'time out', give an estimated time when you will be ready to discuss things. This will help your partner respect your need to be alone.

Acting as if you are short of time

The pain of discovery is often so overwhelming and the sense that your whole life has been destroyed so strong, that it is not surprising that some people want the pain to go away as quickly as possible. When Carl, thirty-eight, discovered his wife of seven years had had a brief affair with a work colleague, he went into overdrive. He phoned his wife's mother and several of his friends to get them to intervene on his behalf. He spoke to his boss, explained the situation, and got a week's compassionate leave. He told his own mother and she phoned his wife too. He researched the problem on the Internet, bought my first book about relationships, and tried to set up an appointment for counselling – before he'd even started reading it. Unfortunately, in his panic, Carl could not properly listen to any of the advice offered. He was too busy looking for what he called the 'killer line' which would convince her to stay, while probably he would have been better just listening to his wife. Worse still, she became enraged by repeatedly receiving calls from worried friends. Later, Carl wished he had not been so free with private information.

Tip: If you feel that you are running against a ticking clock, find a personal positive statement that you can repeat during times of stress. Examples would include: 'I will get through this' or 'We'll come out the other end with a stronger and better relationship.' If nothing springs to mind, keep reading this book as it is full of reassuring advice and examples of couples who have won through.

Pushing for a promise that is hard to keep

When someone is in pain and looking for a quick fix, it is likely they will press their partner to promise something. This is normally to *never* contact the third party again, but I have had clients who demanded their partner give up a job after an affair at work. These promises are readily given because the Discovered wants to feel better and to please their partner. Unfortunately, they are hard to keep.

This is the experience of Margaret, who is forty-seven, and whose husband had an affair: 'He begged me to take him back, which was asking a huge amount from me. In return, I asked him not to have any more contact with her ever again. He promised and immediately failed to keep this promise. When I was away with my sister, he drove all the way to Gloucestershire to talk to his mistress about their break-up. Not only did he keep this a secret from me but he also told our eldest child and told her not to tell me. This seemed like the biggest betrayal of all.' At this point, she kicked him out of the house – threatening him with a knife. 'I was at my maddest and lowest ebb and we parted for a year.'

Although it is unpleasant to think about, the Discovered has spent a significant amount of time with the third party and will have feelings – however inappropriate – for this person and therefore will feel obliged to explain their decision. Worse still, the Discovered feels enough of a 'bad person' without leaving the third party high and dry. This is why a promise of 'no contact' often sets up further clandestine meetings between the ex-lovers which, when discovered, cause more pain than the original betrayal.

Tip: Instead of extracting a promise – which has been framed by you – try negotiating with your partner. How would he or she suggest ending the affair? Where? By letter, by phone or in person? Look at all the details, negotiate and strike a bargain that works for both of you. I would not recommend listening in on the conversation, as this will not only be painful but also inhibit your partner (and possibly set up the need to meet privately with the third party to explain properly). The other problem with a very restricted final contact is the third party will feel 'she's making you say that' or 'he's pulling the strings' and, worse still, the third party will think your partner does not mean to end it and will keep phoning or driving past.

Underestimating the strength of your position

Having an unfaithful partner is never good for the self-esteem. 'I couldn't function at work, as I kept bursting into tears over the slightest thing,' explains Lucinda who is fifty-five, 'I had to go to the doctor for anti-depressants. I feel weak, stupid and unable to cope. All the things that I hate.' With this mindset, it is easy for the third party to seem strong, clever and attractive. In fact, Lucinda could not understand why her partner still wanted her. Time and again, I find that the Discoverer feels vulnerable when it is, in reality, the third party who is powerless. If you are married, own a house or have children together, you are in a strong position. Nobody, however infatuated, gives up lightly under these circumstances. Of course, you do not want your partner to stay just because his or her family will be upset or for the children's sake alone – but this status buys time to try and save the relationship and at this point that is all that counts.

Tip: If your self-esteem is in tatters, think about other things – beyond your relationship – which make you feel good about yourself. This could be your job, being a good father or mother or playing a brilliant round of golf. Set aside time and put energy into one of these areas. Write the best report for work ever, treat the children to a day out at a theme park or take a lesson with a golf professional. Any activity that allows you to immerse yourself in the moment and take a break from your problems.

Coming to a decision on the future too quickly

This stage in the recovery process is about asking questions and discovering the depth of the problem and the extent of both the Discovered's involvement with the third party and the Discoverer's pain. It is not about making long-term decisions. Committing too quickly to saving the relationship often leaves one partner doing all the work – as Melissa, forty-five, found out: 'I've told him I am exhausted and need him to do something for me now. Especially as he has never even apologised. However, he says he's not sure if he can. He just sits there looking helpless while I try and make it work on my own.' Conversely, throwing your partner out sends a message that the relationship is over, when this might not necessarily be your intention. It can also create an unnecessary ticking clock. 'I got fed-up with living out of a suitcase,' explains Marcus, forty-one. 'I also needed somewhere for my daughter from my first marriage to stay at weekends so I visited estate agents and looked for somewhere to rent. When I was on the point of signing, my wife phoned and begged me not to sign – yet she wasn't ready for me to move back in again. I was torn in two, I'd found the first flat that was not only big enough but was also at a rent that I could afford, yet I really wanted to be back at home.' Marcus was already incredibly emotional – forever crying and feeling guilty – this drama not only added to his problems but was also a distraction. While he and his wife were debating the pros and cons of a six-month lease, they could have been tackling the main issues: why did he have the affair, could this marriage be saved and what kind of relationship did they want in the future?

At the moment, you will be filled with all sorts of contradictory feelings: love and hate, hope and despair, fear and relief. This is normal. Unfortunately, we don't like living with ambivalence and push ourselves to coming down on one side or the other – even if it makes things worse rather than better. However, engaging with the complexity of your feelings – rather than rushing into making a judgement – is a skill that is useful not only for your journey from discovery to recovery but also for life in general. Rest assured, it will get easier and the feelings less extreme – but for the time being try and accept uncertainty. It is not necessarily your enemy.

For the Discovered: Intense Questioning

- This is a time of soul searching not only for your partner but also for you: how do you really feel about your lover?

- Discovery throws a spotlight on to your extra-marital relationship and changes everything. Therefore it is not unusual to be confused or uncertain.

- Share your thought processes and emotions with your partner – even if you are still confused and uncertain.

- Keeping your thoughts private might seem kind (why cause more pain?) but, in the meantime, your partner will expect the worst. It is also harder for him or her to understand your final conclusion if you have not shared how you got there.

- Don't be afraid to ask your partner questions too. You will probably have underestimated the depth of her or his feelings about your relationship.

- If your partner asks a direct question about your affair, always tell the truth. Anything less prolongs the Intense Questioning stage and makes recovery harder.

- If you dissemble, your partner will be suspicious and become doubly determined to get an answer – by either further questioning or detective work. When he or she finds the missing information – the results will not be pleasant.

- After the discovery of infidelity, all the old rules in a relationship change. Unfortunately, some people who have been unfaithful do not realise the full implications of their infidelity. They keep back information which under normal circumstances might be forgivable – like porn on the computer – but post-discovery these 'sins of omission' become more proof that 'you cannot be trusted'.

> - Every fresh discovery will remind your partner of the original betrayal. As one respondent to my 'Adultery in the UK' questionnaire enquiry explained: 'Each time was like a body blow.'

New skill: Understanding

The main thrust of Intense Questioning is to understand why your partner has been unfaithful. Although circumstances change from couple to couple, the causes of affairs can be summarised with the following equation:

Problem + Poor Communication + Temptation = Infidelity

Starting with the *problem*, there is nearly always some background trigger point. This can be external to the relationship (like redundancy, bereavement, mid-life crisis) or central to the relationship (feeling unloved, taken for granted, poor or non-existent sex life or a new baby). On their own, these problems are not enough to trigger an affair. However, if someone feels unable to talk or has tried and has not been properly heard, the feelings of despair and hopelessness expand. The relationship might seem okay on the surface but *poor communication* has put it in real danger. When a third party shows interest, provides a listening ear or some other form of *temptation*, infidelity is almost inevitable.

It is easy to put *all* the blame on your partner – after all, he or she systematically lied to you and betrayed you. However, as this formula shows, infidelity is more complicated. Conversely, you should not take all the blame yourself either. You are not responsible for solving your partner's problems, nor are you responsible for keeping her or him away from all forms of temptation. The aim of the Intense Questioning stage is to assess the degree of personal responsibility for what happened. For this, the focus is on the middle of the equation: *poor communication*.

Why do you find it difficult to talk to each other? How good are you both at listening? What is your part in the problems? How could you be different? Although it might seem easier or comforting to picture yourself as the innocent party, this puts you into the victim role. By contrast, understanding your role in the breakdown is empowering and provides either the first building blocks for a plan to rescue your relationship or the opportunity to learn and move on.

To help start the process of understanding, it might be helpful to know the most common factors that increase the chances of someone being unfaithful. According to a 2004 study, reported in the *Journal of Marital and Family Therapy*, they are: a long-standing fear of conflict, a high need for the approval of other people, compartmentalising (dividing life into different sectors), self-absorption (failure to take other people's needs into consideration when making decisions), fear of being abandoned, long-standing low sexual or physical self-esteem and disputes over autonomy and control. The notable themes for the partners of people who had been unfaithful were: perfectionism (which encouraged their partners to avoid conflict), being a mediator during their child-hood (so that, as an adult, they continued to smooth over rather than address problematic areas), fear of abandonment and low self-esteem.

Summary

- The first six months following the discovery of infidelity is the golden window for rescuing a relationship. Do not be panicked into making a decision about the future too soon.
- The main goals of this stage are getting at the truth, and understanding.
- Excessive rage or blaming might temporarily relieve pain but it can make your partner defensive, placating or deceitful and keeps you stuck at the Intense Questioning stage.
- Although it is understandable to want to know the details of the affair, do not keep the focus solely on the third party. This will stop you thinking about your own relationship.

- Common mistakes include rushing to make things better, underestimating the strength of your position, and dismissing the third party's feelings (which can encourage revenge or hamper your partner from making a proper end to this relationship).
- An important element of understanding is to assess your own contribution to the crisis.

Exercises

Coping with the stress

For many people, discovering their partner's infidelity is the worst thing that has ever happened to them. Therefore, it is easy for the stress to multiply and spin out of control. The following will help mitigate some of the effects:

1. *Recognise the signs.* Emotional symptoms include: constant irritability with other people; difficulty making decisions; difficulty concentrating; an inability to finish one task before rushing on to another; feeling unable to cope; loss of a sense of humour; suppressed anger; wanting to cry at the smallest problem; and insomnia. Physical symptoms include: food cravings; lack of appetite; indigestion; nausea; constipation or diarrhoea; muscle spasms and cramps; breathlessness and headaches.

2. *Think of previous times when you have been stressed.* What has helped in the past? What strategies could you use again?

3. *Focus on the next few days or weeks.* Stress increases when we worry about what will happen at Christmas, the Summer Holidays or the rest of our life. Generally, we can cope with right now, tomorrow and the weekend. So focus on short chunks of time and whenever you begin worrying about the distant future (anything more than a month away), bring your mind back to today.

4. *Simplify your life as much as possible.* Take a look at your responsibilities, projects and day-to-day tasks. What could be postponed? What is unnecessary? What could you delegate or give to other people? Who could have the children for the day? Anticipate problems in the next few days and plan around them.

5. *Look at what help is available.* Do you need compassionate leave? There is no need to go into details – a family crisis is sufficient – but make your employers aware that you have problems and will be unable to take on extra responsibilities at the moment. Are there friends or family members in whom you can confide?

6. *Think carefully about whom you tell.* Ask yourself the following questions: Would this person rush to judge my partner? Do I want to talk about private information that would make it hard for my friend or family member to have a good relationship with my partner in the future? Is this person quick to give advice or likely to push me into making decisions and thereby multiply my stress?

7. *Take time out.* This could be sitting in the garden for five minutes and listening to the birds, stopping for a couple of minutes and doing deep-breathing exercises or hailing a taxi cab and being driven aimlessly around for fifteen minutes. Anything that allows you to step off the treadmill for a while.

8. *Enjoy moments of temporary refuge.* It is not helpful to be constantly thinking about the affair, so welcome the distraction that bringing up children or a particularly complex project at work affords.

9. *Acknowledge the stress in your partner.* Go back over the list of symptoms and assess whether your partner is suffering too. Are you making things worse? For example, wanting to talk about problems at 3 a.m. or pressing for some 'commitment' when the focus should be on getting through the next few days.

10. *Take responsibility for your part.* We are most stressed when everything feels out of our control. However, stress

is reduced when we are working towards a goal which is within our power. So think about your contribution towards your marital problems and what changes you would like to make to your own behaviour – rather than trying to change your partner.

Doing a self-audit

This exercise is designed to help you find a middle way between placing all the blame on your partner and, conversely, taking all the blame yourself.

1. Thinking of communication, how good are you at:
   a) sharing your problems with your partner
   b) listening to your partner?

2. Staying with communication, how good are you at:
   a) telling your partner what you like about them
   b) telling your partner about what you do not like?

3. Thinking about your time, energy and attention, where would you place the following in order of priority?
   a) Your job
   b) Your children
   c) Your partner
   d) Chores around the house
   e) TV/computer
   f) Hobbies
   g) Family and friends

4. Looking back at the list above, in which order might your partner have thought that you rank them?

5. Thinking about your sex life, which of the following statements apply?
   a) I did my utmost to keep it interesting and rewarding.
   b) It was a low priority.

   c) I seldom made the first move.

   d) We shared responsibility for initiating sex.

   e) I communicated what I liked and needed in the bedroom.

   f) I found it difficult to talk about my desires.

6. Write down three important contributions that you make to your relationship.

7. Write down three areas where you could have done more.

8. Write down one thing that you would like to change.

9. How could you turn this aspiration into a small, repeatable piece of behaviour? For example, if your change is to talk more, commit to seeking out your partner when you return home and to discussing your day. If your change is prioritising time alone together, you could initiate new bedtimes for the children and stick to them.

How to talk about sex

Having spent twenty-five years as a marital therapist, I know sex is a difficult topic for most couples. This is because talking about our desires creates an unfortunate double whammy. We not only feel incredibly exposed but also sound like we are criticising our partner. So here are some techniques that I use to facilitate a productive conversation.

1. *Finding the language.* In my counselling room, couples often try to discuss sex in a very general way. So general, that I often have no idea what they are talking about. The problem is that they have no words for body parts or sexual practices without sounding like a crude schoolboy, a tabloid journalist, a pornographer or a doctor. There is no easy answer but I think it best to use the correct medical language: penis, vagina, clitoris, breasts, orgasm, sexual intercourse, masturbation and oral sex. This cuts down the

confusion where 'making love' can mean different things to different people and reduces the embarrassment of saying 'dirty' words out loud.

2. *Laughter*. When I was doing my couple-counselling basic training, we always knew which groups of students were doing sex therapy from the waves of hysteria coming from the other tables in the college dining room. There is something funny and ridiculous about sex. When it's done properly, sex brings out the playful, childish, creative parts of our personality. It is supposed to be fun.

3. *Where*. Don't talk in the bedroom. It can easily seem like a post-mortem and never talk directly after an unsuccessful attempt to have sex. This will quickly dissolve into self-loathing or angry outbursts. If you wish to reassure your partner, a hug, fondling, stroking, or a cuddle will be much more effective. Talking in public is equally problematic. Although I do not encourage it, friends or acquaintances have told me about their sexual problems in bars and coffee shops. On several occasions, they have turned round and realised that someone at the next table was listening. On others, we have had to drop our voices to a whisper which makes sex seem a dirty or shameful subject. It is not. Good places to talk include at home or on long car journeys. The latter is particularly productive as it is hard for one person to storm off.

4. *When*. I am not a great fan of making an appointment to talk about sex with each other. It provides time to become anxious or defensive. However, some planning might be needed to make certain that the two of you are alone and unlikely to be interrupted. A good time would be after eating a meal together. You are both relaxed and have a sense of each other's mood. A glass of wine might help loosen the tongue but don't tackle sensitive subjects when you are inebriated.

5. *Taking stock*. To get a sense of how you both feel about your sex life, look at the following question and write your responses separately. (Underneath, I have written the percentages of the population who answered the same in the British Sexual Fantasy Research Project. This will give you a chance to compare your sexual satisfaction and hopefully feel reassured.)

How would you describe your sex life?

Extremely satisfactory
Quite satisfactory
Reasonable
Mediocre
Quite unsatisfactory
Entirely unsatisfactory

(Extremely satisfactory: 19 per cent; Quite satisfactory: 25 per cent; Reasonable: 18 per cent; Mediocre: 12 per cent; Quite unsatisfactory: 10 per cent; Entirely unsatisfactory: 11 per cent.)

6. *Take responsibility*. It is easy for any conversation about sex – however carefully conducted – to sound like criticism. However, this is significantly reduced if you only use 'I' statements. For example: 'I am often frustrated' or 'I would like things to be different'.

7. *Be open-minded*. You might hear something that makes you feel uncomfortable but avoid rushing to make a judgement. Hear your partner out. Get clarification. Ask questions. However, reserve your response until at least you have had the chance to sleep on it. Remember there is a big difference between fantasy and actually doing something. The British Sexual Fantasy Research Project revealed that 33 per cent of the population imagine themselves in a submissive role, 29 per cent in a dominant

or aggressive role, 25 per cent being tied up, 23 per cent tying someone up, 17 per cent being blindfolded and 17 per cent blindfolding someone. Despite the popularity of these fantasies, they remain minority pursuits.

8. *Reaffirm each other*. It is a basic human need to feel loved, desired and sexually potent. So end your discussion with some positive feedback about what you like about each other's bodies and the moments together that give you the most sexual pleasure. Afterwards enjoy a cuddle – preferably lasting a few minutes – as this is a time when touch is more comforting than words.

(Later in the book, I will return to the subject of sex and how to progress discussion into action. However, at this point, it is enough to take stock of your love life, understand what might have gone wrong, and be ready to make an informed choice about the future.)

Checkpoint

Three key points for surviving Stage Two: Intense Questioning

1. Don't panic and rush into making decisions too soon.
2. Explain why honesty is so important to you.
3. Seek to understand why your partner was tempted and why communication between the two of you has broken down.

Stage Three:
Decision Time

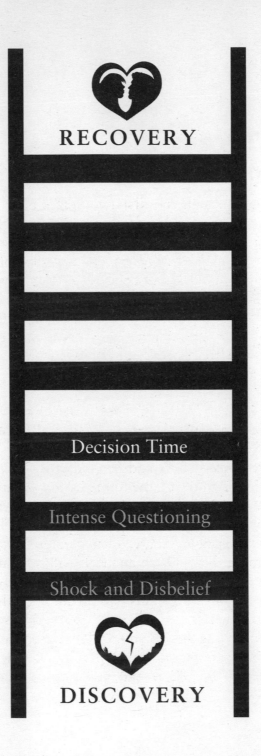

RECOVERY

Decision Time

Intense Questioning

Shock and Disbelief

DISCOVERY

Many people go through the first two stages after discovering infidelity on instinct, autopilot or pure adrenaline. However, by Stage Three, Decision Time, it is time to take a step back and become more rational. Instead of the millions of questions, there is just one: Should I stay or should I go? If your partner has already taken this decision out of your hands, it becomes: Should I accept his or her choice or should I campaign to save the relationship? These are such incredibly important decisions – in fact, life-changing – that it is easy to be overwhelmed. So where do you start?

Eight types of infidelity and the infidelity ladder

Although the feelings of hurt and betrayal are similar whatever the circumstances of infidelity, the future of your relationship will be greatly affected by both the type of affair that your partner has had and the seriousness of it. This next section looks at the eight different kinds of infidelity, their common characteristics and how to combat them. Often an affair will start at the milder end of infidelity but, if unchecked, become increasingly dangerous and harder to overcome. I call this process climbing the 'infidelity ladder'. Knowing where your partner is on this scale is also important. It will ensure that you do not downplay the seriousness of the affair – in the hope that this will minimise the damage to your relationship – or, just as bad, panic, overreact and make poor choices.

1. Accidental

One of the most common laments from people who have been discovered cheating is: 'I didn't set out to have an affair.' They imagine this will make their partner feel better, although it seldom does. However, this defence does beg the question: can someone be unfaithful by accident? If your partner has used this excuse, the natural reaction is to snort with derision. Yet it is surprisingly easy for two colleagues or friends to slip from innocent friendship into an affair without being aware when they crossed the line.

A good example of this phenomena is Philip, thirty-nine, who worked from home and collected his son from school: 'There's a café opposite the gates and one day Jackie – who is a friend of my wife's, and we often socialise [with her and her husband] as two couples – suggested a coffee. I can't remember what we talked about – but nothing really personal. I can't remember if I told my wife every time I saw Jackie but she was aware that we would occasionally meet up and my wife would pass messages to her through me.' About six months later, Philip and Jackie's friendship became more intense. 'She was having a lot of marital problems and wanted a male perspective, so we started talking on an emotional level. At one point, she started crying. Her hand was on the table and I took hold of it and squeezed. There was a bolt of electricity and we both became incredibly shy.'

At the time, Philip downplayed the whole incident. 'I told myself I was imaging things.' So when Jackie asked him to call round at her house – rather than at the café by the school gates – he did not think of it as out of the ordinary: 'She told me there were things she could not talk about in public. At first it was just like the other times, but I knew she was building up to something. I was right. She said that she had feelings for me and then she kissed me. Fifteen minutes later, we were in bed together. Afterwards, I felt terrible. I tried to stop it but I was worried that Jackie might tell my wife.' They had sex on half a dozen occasions and Philip was trying to 'cool things' when his wife found out.

So when did Philip cross the line: going for coffee on a regular basis? Listening to Jackie's problems? Offering comfort to someone in need? Going round to her house when the children were not around? Not telling his wife about this rendezvous? Not leaving when Jackie said that she had feelings? When he allowed himself to be kissed? Or was it only when he went upstairs with her?

Another example is Tania, thirty-four, who had been married for eight years when her husband's work took her abroad: 'We met a couple introduced to us by my sister-in-law. We quickly became good friends, all four of us. However, as we all became closer, I noticed he started flirting with me, which I found flattering. I honestly did not think about starting a relationship with him but I guess I must have encouraged him enough to continue. Over the next year and a half, I gradually became closer to him than her. Finally, he told me about his true feelings for me. By this stage, I felt equally attracted to him and just let it happen.'

'Accidental affairs' often start at work. With the excitement and adrenaline of working as a team on a big project, the sheer amount of time spent together can easily overspill and distort natural emotions into sexual chemistry. Business trips are another curse. If someone travels alone they can become lonely and end up socialising more than normal with colleagues. It is also quite common for Accidental affairs to start at a work leaving do. Perhaps it is the alcohol or the expectation that two people will not see each other again but one party lets down his or her guard and the sparks fly.

Common characteristics
- Short-term. They can be anything from a one-off to about eight weeks long and do not necessarily involve sexual infidelity but stop just short with kissing and cuddling, exchanging flirty emails and keeping secrets.
- They often end when one of the 'lovers' confesses to their partner or becomes so reckless that they are almost begging to be found out.
- Generally, the risks, the guilt and the deceit involved in an Accidental affair outweigh the pleasures.

- This kind of affair should still be taken seriously. There have to be some relationship problems or the seeds of an affair would fall on fallow ground.
- The underlying issues are either relatively minor (for example, 'being taken for granted' or 'too busy to spend enough time together' or 'not talking enough') or so deeply buried that the person who strayed is not properly aware of them (for example, their father or mother fought bitterly and destructively, never argued at all or divorced when they were young. In all these circumstances, your partner would have had no role model for sensibly resolving differences).

What to do?

If your partner has had an Accidental affair, the likelihood is that your relationship has been on autopilot. While one or both of you have been concentrating on work or the children, communication has dropped down to the bare basics. Take the example of Philip and his wife: if they had routinely been talking more, she would probably have spotted how much time the embryonic lovers were spending together and stepped in. Hopefully, the second stage of the recovery process – and all the talking involved – will have sharpened up your communication skills. However, it is important to set aside a regular time to discuss the small events of the day. It only needs to be a few minutes but long enough so that you can share the shape and the emotions of each other's life. This could happen over a meal together, whilst preparing for bed or when you're first at home together. You will need each other's undivided attention, so switch off the TV or computer and explain to the children that this is Mummy and Daddy time.

If your partner keeps on justifying or trying to minimise his or her actions, use the ABC of good communication: A is *address* his or her feelings or opinion ('I know that it only lasted a short while'); B is for *bridge* ('But' or 'However' or 'From where I'm sitting'); C is for *communication* ('I wanted to be treated like that myself' or 'I still feel devastated'). This will allow your partner to feel heard – and so not shut down – but still enable you to get your message across.

Infidelity ladder

Many affairs might start as Accidental but, if there is a serious problem in the core relationship, they will quickly turn into the second kind of infidelity: 'Cry for help'. If an affair brings pleasure or sexual release (particularly where there is a low-sex or no-sex relationship), it can settle into something long-term like 'Self-medication' (see page 84). Finally, there is the risk that the partner who was not unfaithful will decide to have a 'Retaliatory affair' (see page 82).

2. Cry for help

In these relationships, both partners generally know that there are problems. These affairs have probably been around for six months or more but the couple are either unable or unwilling to talk about them. Generally, one partner will bury his or her head in the sand and hope to tough it out. Unfortunately, the other partner is left feeling very alone and, in the bleaker moments, trapped in a hopeless situation. They soon become vulnerable to a third party's advances or, while looking for something to distract themselves from day-to-day misery, begin flirting with friends or work colleagues.

An example of a Cry for help affair is Geraldine who had a very difficult pregnancy which involved several long stays in hospital. The delivery was even more traumatic. 'My abiding memory was Sean trying to sneak away. It was like he could not bear to be there. He let me down so badly that I didn't know if I could forgive him.' Not surprisingly, she suffered from post-natal depression and, although treated by her doctor, remained weepy and emotional. Meanwhile, her husband Sean buried himself in his work and hoped that time would heal their problems.

When her maternity leave finished, Geraldine returned to work where she started an intense friendship with a colleague. It reached the point that they would send each other several long text messages every evening. Sean takes up the story: 'I soon became curious and challenged her. Geraldine told me he was "just a friend" and I sort of believed her.' The texting continued and Sean became curious. 'She had become negative, critical and had started avoiding me. I went through her phone when she was in the bath and it was all there. I was so shocked, devastated and ashamed that I drove around in the car for an hour or two. When I came back, I confronted her with the evidence. I think she was quite relieved.' Although Sean had known that Geraldine was unhappy, he had no idea that it had reached this point. Although Geraldine had not set out to use the affair – which fortunately had not become sexual – as a way of getting Sean's attention, it had just this effect, and the couple started counselling.

Many Cry for help affairs start on the Internet. Perhaps it is the anonymity, the fact that you don't even have to leave your own home and the other people in the chat room are just screen names, so it often does not feel like really cheating.

'We were both fans of the TV show *Lost* and exchanged theories about the plots. He was funny and clever and we started chatting and I sent him a picture,' explains Justine, twenty-nine. 'My relationship with Ian had become very stale but he thought that I was too demanding. So this guy and I talked more and more. I found I could really open up. Be myself. He lived in a city about an hour and a half away by train and I planned to go up there for the day.'

Ian, who is also twenty-nine, knew about this 'friendship' and did everything in his power to dissuade Justine from going. 'I just had to find out if my feelings for this other guy were real or not,' she explained. She met her Internet 'friend' and they had sex. 'Afterwards, I realised that I'd made the biggest mistake of my life and crept home with my tail between my legs. Ian and I had the most terrible row and then ended up talking – probably more than we'd ever talked before.' They agreed to go for counselling where, after many twists and turns (more about this later), they discovered that their relationship had been drifting. 'I was almost thirty, I wanted a proper commitment. I wanted marriage and children, the lot. But I don't know if I'd have admitted it to myself, let alone challenged Ian, if we hadn't been through these terrible months.' It was almost as if the cry for attention had come, in this case, from Justine's unconscious to stop her from burying her true needs.

Common characteristics

- Just like Accidental affairs, these are not necessarily sexual.
- It is generally the first affair and only happens after one partner has tried to express their hurt but felt it has fallen on deaf ears.
- The hallmark of the Cry for help affair is that the person who is being unfaithful makes little effort to cover his or her tracks. In fact, she or he might unconsciously go to great lengths to be found out – like leaving receipts around or phoning the third party on the home phone (even though the number, frequency and length of calls will appear on the bill). When discovered, they make a full confession.
- Often there is an easy-to-spot trigger for the affair – for example, a job loss, post-natal depression or the youngest child going off to university.
- Being unfaithful is often completely out of character and afterwards the deceiver cannot really believe what she or he has done. They are full of guilt, shame and remorse.
- When the affair has been very physical, it is almost as if the deceiver is saying 'notice my sexual needs' and 'I want to show you how important they are to me.'
- The underlying problem is usually fundamental and involves something that normally the couple would be unable or unwilling to focus on.

What to do?

Although this way of asking for help is completely destructive, and highly risky, positive things can come out of this type of affair. When a couple is prepared to truly look at their relationship, they normally find a lot of energy and determination to fix the problems. The other good news is that when couples are finally ready to face their big issue, it often evaporates or is sorted quite easily. This is because the more that a topic is unmentionable, the more power it accumulates until the fears become out of all proportion to reality. Unfortunately, many couples in Cry for help affairs try and paper over the cracks or become side-tracked by fighting over particular details of the betrayal. If you recognise this kind of affair, whether you are the deceived or the deceiver, you need to find the strength to face the problems head-on. Rehearse by writing a letter, imagine it is to someone who will understand and forgive anything. For this reason, you can be completely open and maybe surprise yourself.

Infidelity ladder

If the warning is not heeded, it is easy for a Cry for help affair to become a necessary part of the deceiver's life and turn into Self-medication (see page 84) or even 'Tripod' (see page 91). At this point, the deceiver will become more adept at covering up their infidelity. They might even feel 'entitled' to their affair because their partner has been so neglectful or uncaring.

3. Retaliatory

These are short-lived affairs and motivated by just one desire: revenge. Sometimes the deceiver will feel 'entitled' to the affair because their partner has been ignoring them – perhaps because of the birth of a child or a heavy work schedule. However, the majority of Retaliatory affairs happen after one partner discovers the other's adultery.

This is what happened when Ian, whose partner Justine had a Cry for help affair, logged on to a chat room himself. 'I wanted to see for myself what it was all about and got talking to this girl. She really understood what I'd been through because she'd caught her last boyfriend having cyber-sex,' he explained. Justine found out about their 'friendship' halfway through their joint counselling and was completely distraught. 'I know I brought this on myself, but how could he? Especially as we were making so much progress. I really think I could lose him and I don't want that,' she told me. Although Ian claimed, at first, that he was not getting his own back, he did seem to be enjoying Justine's distress. After a couple of weeks, however, Ian admitted he had been foolish: 'The other woman was talking about flying over and meeting me. Suddenly, I realised that I didn't want to see her. I only wanted

Justine. I've only ever wanted Justine.' It was almost as if this couple needed to sink down into another level of adultery hell, before they could truly open up to each other. The rest of the counselling was straightforward and they decided to get married and truly commit to each other. In this case, a Retaliatory affair had a happy ending but most people are not so fortunate.

Frank and Alice were both in their early forties when they came into counselling, after he discovered her affair. 'What makes me the most angry is not that she has lied and cheated and betrayed me, but that I had hundreds of offers but turned them down because I love my wife,' he explained. Frank was a cameraman and often went away to exotic locations for a few days at a time. I was not surprised that he used the next trip away to sleep with another woman. Alice takes up the story: 'He couldn't get home soon enough to tell me.' 'How did you react?' I asked. 'It's pathetic. I've lost what little respect I had left for him.' Frank had gained no satisfaction from his extra-marital sex and Alice's cold reaction had made him even more depressed. A few weeks later, Alice asked for a divorce and they ended their counselling.

Common characteristics
- The person who has been unfaithful thinks that, if she or he wounds their partner, they will feel better themselves. It is a high-risk strategy that often backfires.
- These are people who find it hard to show the full extent of their anger, or talk about it, so have to find some sneaky way to let it out. This is classic passive aggressive behaviour.
- The affair is often about bolstering a low self-image and making the deceiver feel attractive and sexy again. For a second, they feel powerful and in control.
- The deceiver will either confess immediately or leave tell-tale signs around.
- It is always quickly regretted.
- A Retaliatory affair offers the illusion of evening the score but generally makes matters worse.

What to do?

The desire for revenge might be a natural human emotion but it is not a very attractive one. If your partner has had a Retaliatory affair, you are faced with two choices: to fight back or to forgive. Fighting back just increases the stakes and encourages further reprisals until divorce seems the only option. Forgiveness is tough but if you offer compassion to your partner, he or she is more likely to be compassionate about your mistakes or failings.

What about the passive aggressive behaviour? This is when someone cannot be angry to your face, so goes along with whatever is suggested but later sabotages the agreement. My advice is to be wary of too quick or too easy agreement on difficult issues. Instead, encourage a debate about an option: 'What should we do about further contact with the third party?'; rather than laying down the law: 'I want you to promise never to speak to them again.' The latter might be your first choice but during a debate your partner might explain: 'I feel that I owe it to her to talk face-to-face about why we have to end' or 'It is his son's birthday next week and I promised him I would go ice skating.' You might not like these replies but it is better to talk through the issues – and hopefully find a compromise – than for your partner to agree to your face but sneak off behind your back.

Infidelity ladder

Occasionally, someone will keep their Retaliatory affair secret; a private solace to help them cope with their partner's perceived insensitivity. Under these circumstances, the affair will either become Self-medication or, if it continues, Tripod. However, most Retaliatory affairs are make or break: either a couple will begin to communicate better or the relationship will break down completely.

4. Self-medication

When couples have long-term problems that have been allowed to fester or are acknowledged but nothing is done about them, the relationship becomes fertile ground for a Self-medication affair.

In these relationships, one or both partners feel trapped by duty, the children, marriage vows, financial circumstances or habit. Worse still, the couple are so far apart that they cannot imagine a way that anything could change for the better and have settled for second or even third best. In a sense, these relationships are 'too good to leave but too bad to stay'.

An example of a life in this kind of limbo is Brendan who is fifty-two and has been married for twenty-six years. He no longer loves his wife but they get on 'okayish'. They have not had sex for seven years, stopped sharing a bedroom four years ago, and lead more or less separate lives. 'I really do not want to hurt anyone, but I am not sure that I can go on pretending that I'm happy.' So how does Brendan cope on a day-to-day basis? The answer, of course, is a Self-medication affair: 'The lady I am spending time with is different to anyone I have come across before. She is just – well, lovely. I've gone to bits over her. Should I just shut up – stop the nonsense and just accept my sexless marriage? I do not know, but I don't think this is how I imagined my life at this point in time.' In the same way that some people use a drink after work to unwind, Brendan has been using his affair to take the edge off his misery. Like all coping strategies, drink and affairs only work in the short term and generally cause more heartache than facing the original problem.

However, the need for a Self-medication affair can run deep. Even after her husband discovered her infidelity, 35-year-old Stephanie continued to see her lover, on and off, for three years. As she admitted, this is partly because she was 'selfish', but mainly because she believed that she needed the affair: 'I'm very tactile and my husband is not. He also doesn't open up as much as I do. I suppose I thought I could cope with it when we were first married, but it's got harder and harder. I have explained to my husband how I want him to be over and over again.' Stephanie's misery was so deeply ingrained, the rush of the adrenaline from the affair so powerful and the distance from her partner so great, that there seemed no other option.

Common characteristics

- Both parties are disappointed and unhappy but have been unable to express it in a constructive way.
- The problems are so deep-rooted and long-running that neither party can really put their finger on when things went wrong.
- Subsequently, the couple have grown so far apart that they are living separate lives. In some cases, the atmosphere is quite calm on the surface but this is because neither partner cares enough to fight.
- Both partners will have used coping strategies to endure an unsatisfactory relationship. The person who has been deceived will probably have been losing themselves in work or getting their need for closeness met by the children. Although this is not as destructive as an affair, it is still neglecting the relationship.
- These affairs generally last for six months or more.
- There could have been infidelity in the past, but the lessons were not learnt or the pain was simply swept under the carpet.
- People in their middle years are particularly prone to this kind of affair. At this life stage, we are faced with the reality of our mortality – perhaps by the death of a parent – and the realisation that we will not conquer the world and that neither our children nor our partner are perfect. Worse still, there is the fear that life will only get worse.
- Therefore, a Self-medication affair is often used to boost self-confidence or reaffirm desirability and potency.

What to do?

At first sight, this seems a tough affair from which to recover. However, it is important to recognise the positives: all the problems are finally out in the open and the full attention of both partners is now concentrated on the relationship. A good way to kick start the necessary changes is to use the flop-flip technique. This is taking your normal way of dealing with a problem (which has proved to be a flop) and doing the complete opposite (flipping it over). For example, if you have always bitten your tongue – say what you think. If you have always exploded – try counting to ten and being rational. If you have always ignored small niggles – like leaving outdoor shoes in the hallway – explain what is irritating and discuss alternative solutions with your partner. Not only will these changes provide a boost to your self-confidence but they will also bring you close enough to begin to address the underlying issues. In cases where couples have never really argued – just occasionally sniped or muttered under their breath – this could mean the first real row. If this is you, do not panic as these are deep-seated relationship problems and sometimes have to get worse before they can get better.

Infidelity ladder

This kind of affair is about in the middle of the ladder. For this reason, affairs on lower rungs, if left unchecked, will grow into Self-medication. This is what happened with Tania who was having an affair with a friend: 'It has not helped to revive the sexual desire for my husband, as I thought it may. It has somehow strengthened whatever was solid in my marriage – by making me more aware of the things I like – but exposed more obviously the failings. I feel that I'm at a crossroads. I feel this moment is absolutely crucial – an excellent chance to reinvent myself.' If the third party is particularly committed or the need for Self-medication becomes entrenched, this type of affair will move up to Tripod or even 'Exit'. With any kind of drug use – in essence this is what a Self-medication affair is about – it is easy to tip into addiction and multiple partners, which is the hallmark of the next type of infidelity.

5. Don Juan and Doña Juana affair

Don Juan is a legendary seducer of woman who first made his appearance in Spanish literature in the seventeenth century. Since then he has appeared in books, plays, operas and epic poems leaving a trail of broken hearts, angry husbands and outraged fathers, but Don Juan always remains unrepentant. These epic characters capture our imagination because they tell us something about our own lives. So it is not surprising that, from time to time, I find Don Juan or his female counterpart, Doña Juana, in my counselling room.

A typical example would be Jake, a handsome man in his mid-twenties who seemed to live on his nerves. His partner, Holly, was slightly younger. They had two children and had lived together since their late teens. He had officially admitted to only one affair but Holly claimed to know of at least twelve. 'I like women. I get on well with them, so if I've got a problem I like to talk it over with a woman,' he explained. 'In pubs?' Holly broke in. Jake did not answer; he counter-claimed: 'She's had an affair too.' Holly came right back: 'But we were on a break.'

The couple explained that they would row about infidelity, until the atmosphere became unbearable and Jake would disappear off to his parents for a few days. When he returned home, they would make passionate love but none of the problems would be discussed. 'Sometimes, I think I can't live with him and I can't live without him,' explained Holly.

Contrary to popular opinion, women can be philanderers too. Mia was not only married, but would normally have a long-term lover on the side plus occasional one-night stands: 'They would give me a buzz, make me feel powerful and desired.' Yet at the same time her affairs seldom brought much joy: 'I remember sitting in one lover's car and just banging my head against the windscreen over and over again.' She would be so gripped with jealousy that she would do hurtful and foolish things: 'I once posed as a potential buyer for another boyfriend's house, so I could be shown around by the agent. There was this wall in the kitchen covered in happy snaps of my lover and his girlfriend on holiday, entertaining friends, looking all smug and pleased with themselves. When the agent wasn't looking, I scrawled CHEAT across them. So my lover would know I'd been in the house.'

Like many female philanderers, Mia had been sexually abused as a child and had a low opinion of herself. Her husband would either look the other way or, when she had to confront him with unwelcome news – such as her becoming pregnant with another man's child – just grunt and walk away. Mia did eventually get professional help but it was a long and complex journey.

As you can imagine, being in a relationship with a Don Juan or Doña Juana is difficult and often extremely painful. However, on the surface, they are outgoing, confident and normally very attractive. It is easy to see why so many people are drawn to them. So how can you tell if your partner, boyfriend or girlfriend falls into this category or if the problem is less serious and simply a cry for help or a life-stage crisis? Look at the following list and see how many seem familiar.

Common characteristics

- At the beginning, DJs (Don Juans and Doña Juanas) besiege their target with attention, flattery and gifts.
- The object of their attraction is almost swept away by the DJ's desire and, because they often feel like they are living inside a movie, they quickly agree to sex. It is normally incredible and the target will feel that there has been a real connection.
- DJs have difficulty coping with stress and, rather than confront problems, they will walk away. This is often when their desire for sex is at its highest. (I interviewed one thirty-year-old man, Daniel, who would ejaculate twenty times a week and had had sex with eighteen people in the previous month – including his partner. I asked why he needed so much. His reply was that it was: 'either because I'm getting tense about something or because I'm randy and don't always want to bother my partner'.)
- They have a desire to escape from or suppress unpleasant feelings and to use sex to achieve this goal. Many seem to have an inner void that can only ever be temporarily filled.
- On the surface, these are confident people but underneath they have low self-esteem and a constant need to prove themselves.

- DJs will often have one-night stands and run several 'affairs' at the same time.
- They have a distorted picture of how their behaviour affects other people. They either consider it a 'private matter' or feel that the other person is overreacting. Daniel described his behaviour as 'a bodily function, like going to the toilet. It doesn't mean much'.
- When confronted by evidence of philandering, DJs either get angry and defensive or become tearful and try to get sympathy (for childhood problems or uncaring former partners). However, there is seldom any long-term commitment to change.

What to do?

It is often harder than you would imagine to end a relationship with a Don Juan or Doña Juana. This is partly because they are always promising to change and partly because the beginning of the relationship was such a buzz. Daniel's partner, Debbie, explained: 'The sex was magical, like every cell in our bodies was vibrating at the same rhythm.' (In a small way, this euphoria is like the high that DJs get from their conquests.) However, it is impossible to live in the past and in the present tense these relationships are profoundly harmful. If you have been dating a short time and have just discovered your boyfriend or girlfriend's DJ-style infidelity, my advice is to learn and move on. If this is not your first DJ, you need to question why you find dangerous men or unfaithful women so attractive. The clue is probably in your relationship with your father or mother. (There is more about this in my book *The Single Trap: The Two-Step Guide to Escaping It and Finding Lasting Love*, published by Bloomsbury.)

What about long-term relationships? Most of the partners of DJs have a very clear idea as to just how bad the cheating has become, but have chosen to close their eyes. I have a lot of sympathy for this approach because the alternatives are not attractive. One alternative is that you can try and negotiate ground rules. Hazel, forty-three, is the partner of a bisexual Don Juan and has accepted his relationships with men – as long as he comes back to her at the end of the evening – but has banned sex with other women: 'I have no problems as long as he tells me what he gets up to, but to start off he would fob me off with "nothing much". But it's better now because we have a laugh about how dirty he has been with other men.' This is not an option that many people would choose but Hazel believes: 'If you love someone you put up with their little faults.' The other alternative is to end the relationship. You have probably threatened to leave before or actually done so, but then have been seduced back with promises of change or pleas for second chances. You will know, from bitter experience, how easily these promises are made and how quickly forgotten.

Infidelity ladder

This type of affair is pretty much at the top of the ladder. With so many third parties, it is unlikely that anyone of them will stick and become a Tripod affair. Don Juans and Doña Juanas seldom end a relationship; it is normally their partner whose patience is exhausted, and so they seldom turn into Exit affairs either.

6. Tripod

This type of affair lasts longer than the other types and normally means much more to both the deceiver and the third party. There can be a variety of reasons for the longevity of these infidelities: the person in the middle cannot chose, she or he is happy with the status quo, or the third party is unavailable. However, the common thread is always durability – after all, in the construction industry, triangles are the structures that can bear the biggest load. So why do so many people find themselves trapped in Tripod affairs?

Perhaps, it is their sheer familiarity. Most people's first ever relationship is a triangle: baby, mother and father. Another reason is that being close to someone is both thrilling and frightening. Humans are social creatures and need loving relationships but this involves the risk of being rejected or being taken over by our beloved. In contrast, a Tripod affair manages closeness by spreading

91

the load! (As Princess Diana memorably explained: 'There were three of us in this marriage; it was a bit crowded.') Whenever the main relationship becomes too intense, the person in the middle can always escape into the arms of the third person in the Tripod – a safety valve where all troubles can be momentarily forgotten. Although the affair will be intense, it is never too intense because the deceiver has prior commitments. Sometimes – as, for example, in the case of the Prince and Princess of Wales – there is a matching his and hers Tripod affair. Just like the other types of affair, this infidelity is serving a purpose; so that even if the deceiver ends one extra-marital relationship, he or she will often start another. As the thrice-married businessman James Goldsmith (1933–97) famously said: 'When a man marries his mistress it creates a job opportunity.'

Jackie is fifty-five and has been married for twenty-one years, but has not had any sexual relations with her husband for over ten years. For the past seven, she has been having an affair with a younger man: 'My affair has improved my life more than I can say, although it was a bit of a roller-coaster at the beginning. I have someone who is a very close friend in whom to confide everything and anything. I have the best sex ever, in all sorts of unusual places. He keeps me younger and happier because I have someone to laugh with. I would be very lonely without him. It keeps me going.' The difference between a Tripod and an Exit affair is that, in a Tripod affair, the lovers cannot imagine a way of being together full-time. Jackie explains: 'It would cause a lot of upset with my children and both his family and mine, plus I am too old to ever have children with him. No one can ever know how close we really are.' I would imagine that her husband is suspicious but has chosen not to investigate further, or knows and prefers not to rock the boat.

Common characteristics

- These affairs normally last for upwards of two years.
- Although, on the surface, the primary relationship of the deceiver will have been reasonably stable, the affair is a shadow that undermines and sucks the life out of it.

- The deceiver will 'love' or 'have feelings' for the third party and they will have fantasised about life together. They will have also engineered weekends and even holidays together.
- Infidelity has moved from a coping mechanism to a settled part of the deceiver's life.
- The person in the middle feels torn between their two lovers but ultimately is unable to give up either the security and status of the long-term relationship or the excitement of the extra-marital affair.
- Modern technology makes it hard to keep affairs secret because credit-card bills, mobile phones and email accounts provide incontrovertible proof. Therefore the deceived often collude by being extraordinarily naive, by shutting his or her eyes to the mounting evidence or just by hoping that the affair will burn itself out.
- At the moment when a Tripod affair comes out into the open, the deceived often feels like the weight of the world has been lifted off their shoulders.
- Frequently there is a history of infidelity or divorce in either the family of the deceiver or the deceived. This could explain why the deceived has put up with a relationship that borders on being, or is, abusive and how the deceiver has managed to 'normalise' his or her behaviour.
- Even when a Tripod affair is revealed, the deceiver will often shuttle between their partner and the third party. In so doing, he or she will make everyone, including themselves, thoroughly miserable.

What to do?

The number one priority after the discovery of a Tripod affair is to end it. However, because the deceiver will have emotional ties and sometimes even children with the third party, this is easy to promise but hard to deliver. Yet it is impossible to solve the problems with the primary relationship when there is a ready-made escape hatch if times get tough. So what's the answer? The first step is to be realistic. Discuss with your partner how he or she suggests winding up the affair rather than imposing your preferred formula. It is better to have all the issues out in the open and to find a compromise together, rather than having everything your way but later discovering that your partner has gone behind your back again. If you are fair and reasonable, there is no reason for further deceit.

If your partner too readily promises to cut all ties, ask if the plan is really workable. He or she will probably offer anything to placate you but once again the truth is better than empty words. Next, expect slip-ups and disappointments. The third party will probably keep contacting your partner and, although he or she can be discouraging, it is almost impossible to prevent someone from, for example, turning up at work. Although it is tempting to explode, this will only encourage your partner to be selective about the information passed on. Keep the lines of communication open and discuss your options: should you tell the third party's partner? Should you instruct a solicitor to write a warning letter?

If your partner is unable or unwilling to give up the third party, let him or her go. I know this is painful, and that you fear handing victory to your rival. However, it is better in the long run. As you will read in the next chapter, there is a strong possibility that the affair will collapse and, over time, your partner will realise his or her mistake. Until both you and your partner are fully committed to working on your relationship, it is pointless to try and save it.

Infidelity ladder
The only consolation of a Tripod affair is that it seldom turns into an Exit affair. There is always something strong in the original relationship and, with patience, this can be rediscovered and built on.

7. Exploratory
We live in a culture that constantly encourages us to compare our possessions, lifestyle and experiences with everyone else. Although this gives rise to high aspirations, it can also leave us envious, dissatisfied and ripe for an Exploratory affair. Such affairs are also

on the rise among people at a life crossroad – for example, reaching forty or with children going off to school – who are questioning their past choices and wondering how things would have been 'if only'. For example, 'if only I had stayed with my first love' or 'I had not got married' or 'I had admitted that I'm bi-curious'.

This kind of affair is a door opener. At one end of the scale, the deceiver may take a look at the world outside their relationship, decide it's not for them, and retreat. At the other, it could be the beginning of a journey that ends with the deceiver leaving. Therefore, it is hard to judge the seriousness of this kind of infidelity.

Exploratory affairs tend to be short term and often sexual in nature. In perhaps half the cases I see, the deceiver is reasonably satisfied with their primary relationship but has an overwhelming curiosity about what sex or life would be like with someone other than their partner. Often these people have married young and have a routine or limited sex life.

The other ingredient for an Exploratory affair is that the deceiver must feel it is impossible to talk to their partner about their desires. 'I had married at nineteen and, being a "good" girl, I knew nothing about sex at all. My husband was Catholic and, although older, knew scarcely any more. So things in the bedroom were rushed, unsatisfactory and occasionally even painful,' explains Sheena who credits her affair with improving her marriage. With three small children, she could not go out to work, so took on piecework at home and became friendly with the man who delivered her materials and oversaw her work. 'I was able to learn things from my lover – who was much more experienced – and gradually, so as not to raise suspicions, I'd introduce these techniques into my lovemaking with my husband.'

Fortunately, her husband never found out but she had a couple of nasty scares. 'I was involved in a minor car accident – just a shunt – on my way back from my lover. There was no reason why I should have been in that part of town and that brought me back to my senses. My children were a bit older, I had started to go out to work and my confidence had grown. There was no reason to continue the affair, so I cooled it and we drifted apart.'

Often the affair settles nothing and the deceiver finds themselves in limbo. The experience has increased general dissatisfaction with their partner but, as many Exploratory affairs remained undiscovered, there is no impetus to work on the relationship. Megan, thirty-three, had been married for six years when she had her Exploratory affair. 'I learnt to appreciate my husband better but I also noticed what I have missed.' She considered telling her husband but knew that if she did he would seek a divorce. 'I have kept busy to distract myself, suppressed my feelings, taken courses of acupuncture and read self-help books.' The result has been two years of depression.

Common characteristics
- The majority of deceivers in Exploratory affairs discover that the grass is not necessarily greener on the other side and learn to appreciate what they have.
- For this reason, it is hard to judge the severity of an Exploratory affair. In some ways, it is similar to a Cry for help affair and can be turned round with some relatively minor changes. Conversely, it can tip a relationship under strain into crisis.
- This is the kind of affair that the deceiver will describe as 'just sex'.
- The deceiver may not know themselves how important the affair has been. It is probably only in hindsight that she or he realises that this was a turning point.
- The partner of someone who has had an Exploratory affair is often demoralised and afraid. Unlike other types of affair, there is no clear-cut way back. It can feel like their partner is not asking them to behave differently but to be someone else.

What to do?
Dealing with an Exploratory affair is very frustrating. As your partner is trying to 'find' herself or himself, rather than complain about your behaviour, the obvious solutions of trying harder or

changing will have little effect. It is also common to feel angry. After all, there are lots of ways for your partner to rediscover his or her youth, boost self-confidence or explore different ways of being which do not involve betrayal! So how do you move forward? I would still concentrate on the issues that you can change – like your own behaviour and communication style – rather than obsessing about what you can't. I would also stop trying to reason or convince your partner that she or he is wrong. You are probably wasting your energy, increasing your personal upset and making him or her even more stubborn. Stepping back, temporarily, will lower the tension in the house and hopefully open up more fruitful discussions.

Infidelity ladder
An Exploratory affair does not inevitably turn into an Exit affair. However, curiosity about sex outside the relationship can easily become a need and, at this point, an Exploratory affair will become a Self-medication affair.

8. Exit
Although some people have an Exit affair because they have fallen in love with the third party, and cannot imagine life without them, the majority are simply sending a clear message to their partner that the relationship is over. Under these circumstances, the couple will have struggled, off and on, to sort out their problems and have either drifted so far apart or become so angry that communication is almost impossible. In many ways, an Exit affair is like negotiating through a loud-hailer: nasty, dramatic and blunt.

Frank and Jenny, in their mid-fifties, had been living separate lives and only really spoke to each other when their daughter and grandchildren visited them. It had been many years since they last made love. 'I've thought for a long time that we should quit while we're both young enough to find someone else but Jenny is Catholic and that's unthinkable,' explained Frank. 'We don't see enough of each other – that's the only problem,' Jenny interrupted. 'It's because there's a big contract on at work and I've had to rent a flat nearby,' said Frank. However, it soon became clear that Frank's contract at work would last at least eighteen months and that he had no intention of giving up his bolt-hole. 'And anyway, having to cope on your own has been good for you. You're more confident,' Frank told Jenny.

My guess was that Frank had effectively already left home and had started counselling – not to save his marriage, but to transfer some of the responsibility he felt for his wife on to me. However, it was only a guess because Frank did not open up and only hinted at his true intentions. On the rare occasions that Frank seemed about to open up to Jenny, she would become tearful – almost to the point of hysteria – and he would placate her. Their sessions were painful and unproductive, so we ended counselling. Six months later, they returned after Jenny discovered that Frank had started an affair with a woman at work. It was almost as if Frank, unable to communicate using words, had sent Jenny a message that could not be ignored. Although the affair quickly petered out, the marriage did not last either.

Martin, forty-two, is another example of someone having an Exit affair. 'Ten years or so ago, my wife and I went through a pretty rocky period. From where I sit now, I think I should have made the break at that point. As I remember, I could have walked then and, looking back, should have; but hindsight is a great thing.' In his opinion, his marriage was 'all over bar the shouting at each other' when he met the third party. As is characteristic of many Exit affairs, Martin does not seem to get much pleasure or joy from his adultery. Rather, it is seen as the lesser of two evils: 'I suppose it might have been easier to suffer, as I put it, as the position I find myself in is going to destroy several lives – even if only for a short time.'

Common characteristics
- There have been long-term problems with the relationship.
- This is probably not the first affair, although previous ones may have only been suspected and not confirmed.
- On this occasion, the deceiver has done little to cover up the affair and when it is discovered shows little contrition.

- The attitude of the deceiver is very cold and he or she will often refuse to answer anything beyond the bare facts of the adultery.
- Their partners will be frustrated and angry, and left with hundreds of unanswered questions. In effect, they are trapped in the previous stage of Intense Questioning (see pages 45–72).
- The deceiver has regressed and is behaving like a self-absorbed teenager. If they are leaving because of a 'soul mate', he or she will be full of manic energy and almost drunk on love. If they are leaving because the central relationship has broken down, he or she will be sulky, uncommunicative and appear depressed.

What to do?

It is very easy to get absorbed in the unfolding drama and to forget to look after yourself. So remember that you are going through a crisis and do not push yourself too hard. Get support from friends and family and find ways to cope with the stress. (Lots of exercise helps, as this burns off some of the worry and helps you sleep better, too.) Be careful not to burden your children with too many details. In the long-term, they will need a good relationship with the parent who is leaving – so do not make them your confidant or go-between.

Infidelity ladder

It goes without saying that this is the top rung. However, an Exit affair does not necessarily mean the end of the relationship. It is possible that it could fall back to an Exploratory affair – and the unfaithful partner returns – or a very extreme Cry for help affair.

Five questions to help you decide on your next move

For many people, understanding the nature of their partner's infidelity and some of the root causes provides the necessary clarity to move forward. If you are still undecided, I have five questions to help and some guidance on interpreting your answers.

1. How much responsibility should you take for what has happened?

Go back to the formula from Stage Two, Intense Questioning: Problem + Poor Communication + Temptation = Affair. With your increased understanding of the type of affair, what have you learnt about the communication between you and your partner? What changes could you make that would benefit the relationship – without compromising your dignity and self-esteem?

Interpreting your answers

If there are constructive changes that you would like to make (for example, listening more, talking more, being more honest about your feelings and needs, spending more time together), then I believe that you should decide to fight for the relationship. If your answer is that there is little or nothing that will improve communication or the changes are self-destructive (for example, watching him or her like a hawk or conversely turning a blind eye), then you should seriously consider the wisdom of continuing.

2. What sort of person is your partner?

Putting aside your partner's behaviour during the affair (and all the selfish, destructive and harmful actions), what kind of person is he or she at their true core? Is your partner kind, thoughtful, hard-working or generous? What other admirable qualities can you come up with? What qualities have made it hard for the two of you to live together?

Interpreting your answers

When looking over the whole course of your relationship – and putting aside both your current disappointments and the honeymoon period when you first met – if your partner is basically a good man or woman, I believe you should fight for the relationship. If your partner has been mainly unfeeling, controlling, neurotic, abusive or violent – with the exception of the honeymoon period when he or she was wooing – then I believe you should think again. If the positives are all about your partner's potential or how she or he behaves in sporadic golden moments (like in the making-up phase after a terrible fight), then I think you should also consider leaving. What counts is the core of your partner's real personality, not how you would like him or her to be.

3. How do you feel about your partner?

Do you like your partner? Do you love or respect her or him? Do you share the same goals and dreams?

Interpreting your answers

Although blind love on its own is not enough to sustain a relationship, if your love is still strong and, most importantly, you also like and respect your partner, then there is something to fight for. Shared bonds and interests are positive, too, and provide a framework on which to build. If your feelings are still strong but incredibly negative – by this I mean feelings such as hatred, anger, desire for revenge – then there is still life in your relationship. However, if your feelings are neutral, cool or indifferent, I doubt there is any drive left to save the relationship. We think that the opposite of love is hate but, in reality, it is apathy.

4. What would be the impact on other people if you split up?

In my on-line survey into adultery in the UK, this was the most important factor for people deciding to fight for their relationships. In fact, 85 per cent of respondents cited the impact on their family. This is no surprise. In a crisis, our natural reaction is to gather up and protect our children.

Indeed, the research backs up our instinct that divorce harms children. In the seventies, Judith Wallerstein, PhD, the founder and executive director of the Center for the Family in Transition in California, decided to study the impact of family break-up. She recruited sixty families with 131 children between the ages of two and eighteen from referrals by lawyers and family courts. As she expected, little children had trouble sleeping, older children had trouble concentrating at school, and adolescents were acting out their pain and anger. The surprise came when she returned for the eighteen months' follow-up. Instead of recovering and getting on with their lives, as she had expected them to be doing, the symptoms of distress were even worse. So Wallerstein decided to follow up her families again – five, ten and twenty years after divorce. Here are her main findings after eighteen months, five years and ten years:

At eighteen months:

- The turmoil and distress of the break-up had not noticeably subsided.
- One third of younger children did not believe what they had been told and still thought their parents would get back together again.
- Only one child in ten was relieved that their parents had divorced. These were older children who had witnessed violence and were frightened that either they or one of their parents would get hurt.

At five years:

- About a third of the children were doing better. These were families where the parents had fought openly and the atmosphere in the house had been miserable. They had also maintained a good relationship with both their parents.

- However, a third of the children in the sample were significantly worse and had become clinically depressed. Wallerstein reported: 'True, some couples were no longer standing in the same kitchen screaming at each other; they were screaming on the telephone instead. Or they fought face to face while dropping off or picking up [their] children. The illusion we had held – that divorce brings an end to marital conflict – was shattered.'
- The majority of children still hoped that their parents would get back together again, even if one or both had remarried. As one child told Wallerstein: 'If they can divorce once, they can do it again.'
- Few of the children were truly sympathetic to their parents or really understood why their parents divorced – even when their parents thought it was obvious.

At ten years:

- Three out of five children felt rejected by at least one of their parents.
- Half of the women and a third of the men were still intensely angry.
- One in four children had experienced a sharp drop in living standards.
- However, half the adults were happy with their present lives and considered divorce a closed book with no regrets.
- Divorce is an unpredictable lottery. 'Some of the most troubled, depressed and fretful children in our study turned out fine ten years later, while some of the least troubled, seemingly content and calmest children were in poor shape,' reports Wallerstein. 'One cannot predict the long-term effects from how they react at the outset.'

Interpreting your answers

If you and your partner have children or complex family ties, I believe splitting up should be the last resort. By contrast, if you have no children and your families will only be sad or disappointed if you separate, perhaps the infidelity is an early warning and that it would be unwise to commit yourself further to the relationship.

5. How committed is your partner to repairing the relationship?

Does your partner beg for another chance? Does she or he seem genuinely sorry and truly to have digested the hurt that has been caused? Do your partner's actions back up his or her words or does your partner say one thing and do another?

Interpreting your answers

If your partner is keen to repair your relationship, this is a definite plus point. If he or she is ambivalent, the task is harder but still possible. Even if your partner has been caught texting or emailing their ex-lover, this should not stop you fighting for the relationship. Ultimately, the question at this point should be: 'What do I want? To fight or to walk away?', not 'If I fight for this relationship, will I be successful?'

Still stuck?

Recovery from infidelity is such a high-wire act that everybody loses their nerve and wonders if they have made the right decision. However, some people get trapped in the decision phase and are unable to find any clarity. If this sounds familiar, it is probably down to one of the following reasons:

- Waiting for a sign from your partner. Either your partner is so mixed up that he or she is unable to give a clear commitment, or words are not enough on their own to convince you. Either way, you need concrete proof that your partner wants to stay before you make your own mind up. If this is you: think about what form the proof might take – for example, a second honeymoon. And instead of expecting your partner to be a mind reader, tell him or her what would help.

- Abdicating responsibility to your partner. Waiting for your partner to make up her or his mind, before you can decide yourself, leaves you in no-man's land. If this is you: it feels risky to commit to saving the relationship on your own – in case you are rejected for a second time. However, the alternative is to be stuck feeling impotent and hopeless. By contrast, fighting for what you want is empowering.

- Trying to work out the pros and cons. It makes intellectual sense to put all the benefits of staying in one column and balance them against the benefits of leaving – rather like using the scales held by the Statue of Justice on top of the Old Bailey in London. Unfortunately, it is impossible to weigh the known qualities of today against the unknown events of tomorrow. No wonder people who are approaching the decision like a judge get stuck. If this is you: try making a diagnosis instead – rather like a doctor – and look for signs of health in your relationship. Is there something worth fighting for? Or are you trying to revive a dead corpse?

For the Discovered: Decision Time

- Since your affair has been revealed, you will have been under a lot of pressure to make a commitment to either your partner or your lover.

- For some people this is a clear-cut decision; however, others are left unable to choose between two very different people.

- If you are undecided, ask yourself: what did my affair mean to me? To help with this process, look at the eight types of infidelity (Accidental; Cry for help; Self-Medication; Retaliatory; Don Juan or Doña Juana – serially unfaithful; Tripod – long-term; Exploratory; or Exit).

- Next, ask yourself: are there other ways of fulfilling these needs? For example, what other ways could I feel good about myself or wanted?

- What would be the consequences of leaving? What about your children? If your lover has children too, what would it be like to be a stepfather or stepmother? Be aware that divorce is not something to which children quickly adjust but, rather, the most important event of their whole childhood.

- Try to avoid shuttling backwards and forwards between your partner and your lover. This is the most painful option for everybody concerned – including yourself. No decision is ever perfect and whether you stay or go, you will have to learn to cope with loss.

- If you're considering taking time away from home to think, be specific about how much. For example, a weekend. Choose somewhere your partner will consider 'safe' – like your parents' house – so your time-out is not viewed as an opportunity for a liaison with your lover.

New skill: Confident and productive decision-making

In the business world, decision-making is something that is endlessly studied. So what can we learn from the management sciences and how do we apply it to personal problems? Good decisions are made when the following conditions are met: all the options are fully considered; the evidence is properly tested; it is done in a timely manner and the goals are well defined.

So let's look at each of these conditions and how they apply to infidelity. First, have you considered all the options? When something is very painful – like splitting up or facing the demons in a relationship – the temptation is to peak into the future and then close our eyes. The result is that people plunge blindly on or shut down an option without truly considering it. They can also overlook halfway options – like sleeping on the sofa or staying with parents for the weekend. In good decision-making, people test the facts rather than assert or assume them. So get legal advice and work out the finances.

It is also important to consider *all* the evidence. Unfortunately, we tend to focus on memories that are most easily retrievable, which tend to be recent or emotional (in other words, heavily dependent on the last few months and overlooking the whole history of the relationship). We also tend to remember evidence that shows us in a good light (researchers call this self-serving bias) or supports our viewpoint (called confirmation bias).

The next test of good decision-making is whether it is done in a 'timely' manner. At one end of the scale, I have counselled people who have leapt too quickly into committing to saving their relationship – when they were still in shock and not in possession of all the facts. At the other extreme, I've seen couples who have not actively decided to stay together but have put off the decision so long that it became a fait accompli. However, for most people, a timely decision will be made somewhere between two weeks and two months after the discovery of the infidelity.

Finally, good decision-making needs 'well defined goals'. These are targeted, specific and measurable. For example, going into couples therapy or having an evening out together once a fort-night, and should be regularly reviewed.

What hinders good decision-making? In my experience, couples who get stuck in this phase tend to use *advocacy* rather than *enquiry* to settle their differences. Advocacy is a contest where each side strives to persuade the other and defends their weak points. The result is that one partner 'wins' and the other 'loses'. Enquiry, by contrast, is about collaborative problem solving. Each partner remains open to alternatives and accepts constructive criticism. The result is that both gain something and both compromise on something.

Summary

- There are eight kinds of infidelity, and understanding which kind of affair your partner has had will help you assess the long-term viability of your relationship.
- An affair can start as one kind of infidelity but over time can change into something more serious and threatening.
- When deciding whether to stay or go, it is better to make a diagnosis about the overall health of your relationship, like a doctor, rather than weigh up the evidence like a judge. This is especially important because people tend to overestimate the duration of the bad times and underestimate the amount of time needed to recover from a divorce.
- It is difficult to make good decisions when you are preoccupied with trying either to second-guess your partner's feelings or to convince your partner to stay (and therefore are unable to listen to your own heart or head).
- Couples often get stuck because, instead of agreeing to try and make their relationship better, the Discoverer is asking for a guarantee that it will work out or the Discovered feels obliged to make such a promise.

Exercises

Coping with the highs and lows

It is hard to make good decisions if you are swinging from euphoria to despair – often for the flimsiest of reasons. To help smooth out some of the highs and lows, try this idea which has been adapted from Buddhist meditation:

- When hit by a wave of panic or despair, stand still with your legs shoulder-width apart or, if possible, find a chair and sit down with your back straight. (If you are somewhere private, close your eyes.)
- Instead of letting your mind race, concentrate on your breathing.
- Feel the air slowly coming in and out of your nose.
- When your mind starts worrying about 'this' or picturing 'that', push the thought away and concentrate on the sensation of air passing in and out of your nose again.
- As you become calmer, imagine the air being breathed out is black negative smoke and the air being breathed in is white and positive.
- Keep going for about five minutes or until you feel more balanced.
- Repeat as often as necessary but, over time, you will find this exercise will get easier and your mind will be a little less overactive.

At the crossroads

When faced with a difficult decision, it is easy to panic and either immediately plump for what at the time seems the easiest option or become overwhelmed by the multitude of choices. This exercise is designed to help you find a middle way.

1. Take a piece of paper and make a cross in the middle. Mark the ends with arrows, to show the different directions from this crossroads.

2. Go round the signpost and give a name to your four options and write them in. If you cannot think of enough, call one 'stay where I am' but try and name all four – even if it is something that sounds unfeasible. If you have more than four options, add extra directions to your signpost.

3. Imagine what it would be like to follow each direction. Close your eyes and conjure up as much detail as possible. Afterwards, summarise your findings about how life would look beside that direction.

4. Finally, imagine a little further into the future in each direction and write down the feelings involved if you made that choice.

5. Accepting that no decision is perfect, which option seems best?

The daily pages

This exercise is designed both to help you locate your inner compass and to cope with difficult times.

- Each day take a fresh piece of paper and write in longhand whatever comes into your head. Do not worry about the punctuation, spelling or grammar. Just write a stream of consciousness.

- It can be extremely banal (did I put the cat out?) or extremely deep (what am I going to do with the rest of my life?). Just write whatever comes into your head and keep going until you have filled your piece of paper. If nothing comes to mind, just put: 'I am writing' over and over again.

- Repeat this exercise every day, or at least five times a week.

- The pages will often be self-pitying, repetitive, childish, angry, silly-sounding or complete nonsense. It does not matter, put them away for now.

- At the moment, the exercise is about draining the excess emotions and not about understanding anything. So keep writing and filing away.

- At the end of the first week, scan over the pages. Do you notice any patterns or particular concerns?

- Keep up your daily pages and by the end of the second or third week, you will find that it is impossible to write day after day without becoming constructive.
- By this point, the exercise becomes a sort of meditation on understanding yourself. You might like to increase the length of your writing from one page to two or three.
- At the end of the first month, look back over all your daily pages. What changes can you see? How has your mood and attitude shifted? How have your feelings towards your partner and his or her infidelity changed?
- The daily pages will bring feelings to the surface during stuck times (when it seems you or your partner are making no progress) and help purge your feelings during difficult times (when you seem always angry with him or her) but, most importantly, a new way of approaching your partner will gradually emerge. Be patient and keep going.
- Do not be surprised if the daily pages reveal new things that initially feel disconnected from infidelity. For example, you might want to start singing, take up running or join a book club. These are all ways of valuing yourself, and will help in the long run.

Checkpoint

Three key points for surviving Stage Three: Decision Time

1. Make certain you have all the necessary information to diagnose the seriousness of the affair.
2. Think through the long-term implications for other people.
3. Concentrate on achieving your preferred outcome. It is better to fight and lose than to give up without trying.

Stage Four:
Hope

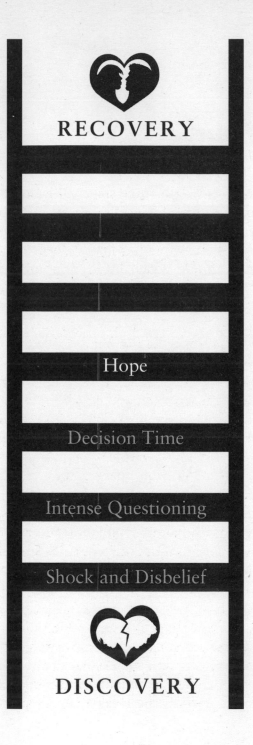

RECOVERY

Hope

Decision Time

Intense Questioning

Shock and Disbelief

DISCOVERY

After the turmoil of the first three stages, it is good to reach the calmer waters of Stage Four. The Discoverer starts to believe that the relationship might just survive the cataclysmic chaos of infidelity. Perhaps the Discovered has finally opened up about some small detail of the affair which he or she had stonewalled or evaded before. Maybe there has been a show of tenderness from the Discovered and the Discoverer feels that their partner really wants to recommit.

'I felt like the blood was finally pumping round to every part of my body again,' explained Anita, forty-eight. 'I know it sounds strange but until you begin to relax that awful watchfulness, you don't realise how tightly wound and closed in on yourself you've been.' Although there can be hope in the first three stages, it is often fleeting or just wishful thinking. In contrast, by Stage Four, hope is based on solid, demonstrable behaviour rather than empty words or wild promises. For some people, these feelings can match the euphoria of when they first met.

However, hope is one of the most fragile of human emotions and this stage is often the shortest and most precarious. If you are still struggling to find any hope for your relationship – perhaps your self-confidence has been knocked or the third party is still on the scene – there is reassurance and grounds for optimism later in the chapter. If you have reached hope but are worried about slipping, there are also strategies for supporting and reinforcing it. However, first, I need to explain why couples can slide back to the earlier stages and reassure that such setbacks are normal.

Anita and her husband Richard had been making good progress with their counselling until the week that Anita found a small teddy bear when putting clean laundry into her husband's drawers. She was immediately suspicious: 'I certainly hadn't given it to him and I instinctively knew that it was a present from her. It was like I was right back at day one when my son showed me a flirty text from her on his phone.' The return to Stage One: Shock and Disbelief was sealed when Richard admitted that it had been a Valentine's Gift. 'I felt like I had been betrayed all over again; just touching this horrible red satin thing made me feel dirty. Not only did I wonder how he could have kept something so tasteless, but I also wondered, if he could fall for someone who thought that a cheap teddy was good idea, what that said about his taste in woman. What does it say about me?' Anita had quickly moved on to Stage Two: Intense Questioning.

Richard tried to explain: 'The present meant nothing. I'd forgotten all about it. Otherwise, I would have thrown it away ages ago.' Anita was straight back on the attack: 'Deep down you wanted to keep it.' It was clear that they had had this argument many times during the week. Worse still, the pain, the unhappiness and the sheer nastiness of their fights had made them question whether their relationship had a future. 'I really don't know if I can ever get over this,' admitted Anita, 'the feelings are so raw. I found myself sitting in the car park at work this morning – shaking. I had to will myself to get out and face the day.' Richard felt similarly despondent and worried about the future. 'It just doesn't get any better. I don't think she'll ever forgive me.' These are typical thoughts from Stage Three: Decision Time. If you find yourself facing similar setbacks, it is often helpful to go back a chapter or stage again.

Fortunately, the journey back to *hope* is quicker the second, third or fourth time around. After much challenging from Anita, Richard finally admitted that, at the time, the present had been important to him. 'I suppose that's why I kept it. However, looking at it now, I wonder how I could ever have thought it was nice. It's mad, really. I can't really understand what I saw in her, either.' So why had he not said this earlier? 'It seemed kinder to tell Anita that it meant nothing. Why rub her nose in it all over again?' Anita was quick to clarify her stance: 'I can tell when you're not being entirely truthful and it brings up all my old anxieties. So I'm really grateful that you've been honest with me now.' During the row about the teddy, Richard had also realised that he was no longer infatuated with the other woman and made an important step forward towards recovery.

How to support and reinforce hope

Whether you are having trouble reaching this stage, are feeling only precariously hopeful or trying to fight your way back to hope again, here are four strategies to help:

Embracing the fragile moment

During tough times, it is easy to be either nostalgic for the past or worried about the future. The hardest place to live is in the present. However, this is the only place that real joy can be experienced. When the playwright Dennis Potter was interviewed on TV shortly before his death from cancer, he was filmed chain-smoking and taking swigs from a hip flask of morphine. His wife was suffering from breast cancer and would die nine days before him.

However, he was still able to find small explosions of joy: 'The only thing you know for sure is the present tense, and that nowness becomes so vivid that, almost in a perverse sort of way, I'm almost serene. You know, I can celebrate life. Below my window in Ross, for example, the blossom is out in full now. It's a plum tree, it looks like apple blossom but it's white, and looking at it [through the window when I'm writing], instead of saying: "Oh that's nice blossom" . . . I *see* the whitest, frothiest, blossomest blossom that there ever could be.' Potter might not have lived to taste the plums but that did not matter because he was living in the fragile moment. Unfortunately, many people struggling with infidelity cannot enjoy their moments of hope – perhaps a family day out by the sea – and the chance to top up their store of good times together. This is because instead of marvelling at the blossom, they are worried that the fruit will rot on the ground.

'Safety-first' living

During the Hope stage, the Discoverer wants to believe their partner and trust again, but it feels like an impossibly giant leap of faith. 'Safety-first' is a contract to bridge the divide. The idea is that the Discovered commits to providing reassurance for the Discoverer by being more open and transparent about their movements and activities. For example, when Jeanette, thirty-eight, had an Internet affair, she offered to move the home computer from the study to the living room: 'In that way, my partner could see that I was on eBay rather than chat rooms. I also cut down the number of hours that I spent online, too, and we'd watch a film together instead.' When putting together your 'safety-first' contract, here are some issues to consider:

- How often should your partner contact you by phone/text/email on an average day? How often is it acceptable for you to contact him or her?
- What level of scrutiny of private communications is acceptable?
- Should your partner call if he or she is going to be late home? How late before there is a need to call? Ten minutes, half an hour, an hour?
- What should happen if there is some contact with the third party? (This is particularly tricky if the affair happened at work. What could be done to reduce the amount of time spent together? What types of conversation are acceptable? What types are not? How much information do you want about this contact?)
- What changes to routine would be advisable or desirable? For example, driving a different way to work or dropping out of a circle of friends, for a while, because these activities were associated with the affair.
- How could you ask for, rather than demand, these changes?

It will probably take several conversations to set up a 'safety-first' contract but this is an opportunity to practise better communication and for the Discovered to make amends. Unfortunately, it is easy to get caught in a downward spiral of blame and defensiveness and the result is despair rather than hope. So how do you avoid this trap?

Choose a moment to talk – when the two of you are reasonably relaxed, rather than straight after a row. It is also important to stress that the changes are *only* for the next few weeks, while confidence and trust is at a low point. For example, after two months, Jeanette's partner Patrick suggested moving the home computer back upstairs as he found himself checking work emails rather than switching off in the evening.

Try and keep intrusion into private correspondence to the minimum – just enough to offer reassurance. Patrick decided to ask for the password to Jeanette's private email – which she had used to communicate with her lover – but not to bother with her work account: 'I didn't want to trawl through the endless memos and office jokes – I get enough at my own office – but mostly I didn't want to come across as a paranoid control freak,' he explained.

Finally, you can ensure the smooth running of your 'safety-first' living contract by giving positive feedback to your partner about how it is helping. For example: 'I really appreciated that call as I'd started to worry' or 'I know that you feel checked up on but I really enjoy chatting about our days together.'

If your partner reveals something upsetting, it is natural to be angry or bitter. However, when you have calmed down, go back and thank him or her. Returning to Anita and Richard, whom I mentioned earlier in this chapter: Richard told Anita that he'd seen his former mistress in the supermarket. This revelation prompted an explosion from Anita. 'She accused me of still fancying her [his lover] and following her, and only telling her [Anita] to cover my tracks,' said Richard. In counselling that week, Richard admitted that he would think twice about future similar disclosures. Fortunately, Anita backed down and asked for forgiveness. 'Actually, I'd been pleased that you had told me but at that moment I had all these negative feelings eating inside me – because you hurt me so much – and I needed to get them out somehow.' By apologising and offering positive reinforcement for honesty, she had kept the 'safety-first' contract alive.

Reconstructing the affair in your mind

Although by this stage of recovery, the majority of the fundamental questions – who, when, where – have been asked and answered, the Discoverer is still left with the 'why' of infidelity. So, at first sight, going over the smaller details of an affair might seem a strange way to prolong hope, but it is an important part of the healing process for both partners. Reconstructing the events allows the Discoverer to put her or his life back together in some semblance of order and to make sense of what has happened. For the Discovered, it is important to understand the full impact of their deception. Answering their partner's questions and making a full disclosure will also unpick the bond with the third party, created by secrets, and help the Discovered understand their own behaviour better. Reconstructing the affair is particularly important when the Discovered is still holding a candle for the third party.

Brian and Tina had been married for eight years and had a toddler when Tina's one-year affair was discovered. Although she readily agreed to end all contact and enter counselling, their progress was minimal. The problem was that Tina still had strong feelings for her ex-lover. 'If I could just flick a switch and fall out of love, I would, but it's not that simple,' she explained. Beyond basic information, Tina had refused to discuss the affair. Her silence allowed the affair to be filed away as something romantic and special. With some encouragement, Brian finally began to push for details: What did she do for childcare when she was meeting up with her lover? How did the other man deceive his wife to get free time? After they finished, I asked Tina for her reaction. 'It all sounds rather sordid and deceitful. I'd had this image of my lover as being kind and honourable but actually he treated his wife appallingly. She trusted him implicitly and he abused it.'

Reconstructing the affair can easily degenerate into destructive rows. So what is the difference between something positive, which can help a couple to move on, and simply dwelling on the pain?

- Reconstructing involves laying down the chronology of the affair against what was happening in your life. How did the affair impact on your life together?
- Reconstructing is about understanding the motives and thought patterns of your partner as the affair progressed. What was he thinking when he took his lover away for the weekend? What was she feeling when she dropped the children off at her mother's for an afternoon rendezvous with her lover? How did your partner and the third party imagine the future?
- Reconstructing is done because of a niggling fresh question that needs answering. Be gentle and afterwards thank your partner for co-operating (after all, it shows that the two of you can work through difficult material together). By contrast, dwelling on the pain goes endlessly over the same ground and punishes either yourself or your partner.
- Reconstructing replaces your wild imaginings with the often-mundane reality of what actually happened.
- Reconstructing can be viewed in a positive light: 'I need to do this to put things behind us' and your partner co-operating is concrete proof that they want to help your recovery.

To take an example of how a reconstruction can help, Julie, thirty-one, was pregnant when she discovered that her partner of four years had been unfaithful. She had gone home early due to ill health from her best friend's wedding and her partner had got talking to a fellow guest: 'I had to know everything in exacting detail – I am an analyst and fine detail is important to me. He slept with her twice in a two-week period and both incidents involved alcohol. For the most part it seemed he was sending text messages and he maintains that he only saw her about five times.' This knowledge helped Julie pinpoint her anger: 'I feel worst about the lies and the betrayal. The fact that he couldn't say no and that it was easier to hurt me than to turn her down. However, I have also seen the actual messages between them and she was quite obviously the protagonist – even though she knew I was pregnant. So a lot of my anger is displaced to her. That might be wrong but she was very persistent.'

So has Julie gone through periods of being hopeful? 'Yes, all the time! The hopeful part is that he is finally opening up to me. He tells me how things feel, in intense and often painful conversations, but we have got down to the root cause of his unhappiness.' They had started living together for convenience rather than out of a positive commitment to each other. 'The hopefulness is that we have a future together and I can see it. It feels like happiness and if I am honest, I haven't felt that for a while either.'

Enjoying the improvement in your sex life

In my survey 'Adultery in the UK', 83 per cent of couples who had reached this stage reported significant improvements in their love life. One woman, fifty-one years old, whose partner of twenty years had been unfaithful, reported sex going from 'once a month, and most times not even that, to three times a week.' Another example is Miranda, forty-six, and her husband, whom she met when they were teenagers; they had been married for over twenty years when he had a four-month affair with a work colleague in luxury hotels. 'I was bored in bed before the affair but could never tell him what I wanted; when our relationship exploded we put it back together in a new way and our sex life was liberated.' This was not an uncommon experience, and 15 per cent of couples in the survey reported, unprompted, that infidelity had encouraged them to try new things in their lovemaking.

So what is behind this phenomenon? For many respondents, sex provides the reassurance that they crave but for others it is something darker – almost as if they are reclaiming their partner.

Peter, fifty-one, reported 'very frantic and passionate lovemaking' after his wife admitted to an affair with an old flame. 'But sometimes, I get turned on by what she's done and imagine it's him, not me, making love to her – this seems so sad and perverted.'

However, I think the real reason for improved sex lives is even more fundamental. There are two parts to our sexuality: *our own inherent sexuality* (what touch excites us, personal preferences, the physical process of reaching orgasm) and *relationship specific sexuality* (chemistry, the give and take between each partner's inherent sexuality, what's happening in the wider relationship). If we have been with our partner for a long time, we become so familiar with our relationship specific sexuality that we lose sight of our own inherent sexuality. However, the rupture of the affair makes each partner step back and remind themselves about their own personal preferences. When this inherent sexuality is reintroduced (what we really fancy) rather than the relationship sexuality (what both partners don't mind), the effect is dynamite.

Paul and Tracey, the couple from the second chapter who rowed after he finally revealed that his inappropriate friendship had been sexual, went through the dark frantic lovemaking stage. 'It was just like the self-help books describe – really intense,' said Paul. 'However, afterwards, Tracey would turn away from me as if she was disgusted and, to be honest, I didn't feel that hot either.'

After a while, their sex life did change into something more positive. How had things changed? It took them a while to put their finger on the difference. Finally, Paul found the words: 'It's more tender. I don't want to climax but make it last as long as possible and afterwards we cuddle together and feel close.' They had also talked a lot about the difference between having sex (which is what Paul called his relations with the other woman) and making love (what they did together).

During these conversations, they found a degree of honesty that had been absent beforehand. 'I often couldn't be bothered,' said Tracey. 'I would sulk if I didn't get sex as often as I wanted,' explained Paul. This increased tension had prompted Tracey to often have a drink to help her get into the mood for making love, which further fuelled Paul's unhappiness: 'It didn't make me feel very special that my wife had to be tipsy before wanting to touch me.' After talking, Tracey realised she should 'make more of an effort' and Paul concluded that 'I'd been really rather teenage and selfish' and their lovemaking became deeper and more meaningful.

So what if you're not getting a sexual bonus? I would check that you have truly reached the Hope stage. If you are not comfortable being intimate with your partner, it is probable that either one of you is, or both of you are, still stuck in decision-making. Be reassured, you are not alone. Seventeen per cent of people in my survey – who had felt hopeful about their future – did not feel ready to make love again. For these people, it is impossible to reconnect sexually before regaining trust – and trust is generally the last ingredient in the recovery from infidelity. In the meantime, I would recommend finding non-sexual ways to be physically intimate: kissing each other when you arrive or leave, casual physical touching (a hand in the small of the back to guide your partner through the door or squeezing a hand at moments of stress) and cuddles (preferably on the sofa or in bed and lasting ten minutes or more.)

By embracing the good times together – however fleeting; by setting up a contract for 'safety-first' living, reconstructing the affair in your mind and enjoying the improvements or the beginnings of a reconnection in your sex life, you should begin to feel hopeful more often and for longer periods of time. (If you still cannot reach the Hope stage, look at the exercise: 'Letting go of blame'.) There will still be dark days when you feel in competition with the third party and worry that your everyday love cannot compete with the excitement of an affair, but even here there are grounds for optimism.

The difference between married love and affair love

Married love ebbs and flows. Sometimes, it is just like when you first met but at others, you are tired, disappointed, bored and even angry. In contrast, affair 'love' could not be more spicy. It is one long, emotional rush – fuelled by danger and secrecy. However, the very things that make affair love so seductive are nearly always its downfall. Affairs always take place in a bubble: an unreal world where it is easy to confuse infatuation for true love and to believe that your feelings will never change.

I am reminded of a story that a young gay friend told me at the end of the seventies. He was dating a member of the Italian nobility with a flat overlooking a park in Central London. They spent their time either in bed or drinking champagne. It all sounded terribly glamorous. Unfortunately, the baron was terrified that someone would find out that he was gay as that would be, to quote my friend, 'social suicide'. (When the baron had been young, homo-sexuality was illegal and gay men were routinely imprisoned.) He claimed to be desperately in love but could not introduce my friend to either his family or his friends and seldom risked being seen out with him in public. He once grandly declaimed, probably fuelled by champagne, 'I can love you, but only as far as the door.' On another occasion, he wished: 'If only we could spend forever here in this bed.' Although there was no third person in this rela-tionship, it was just like an affair: secret, confined and obsessive.

So what happens when the person who has been having an affair decides to go public, or is discovered, and declares his or her new love for everyone to hear? In theory, the affair should emerge from the shadows and the new couple ride off into the sunset. However, it is never that simple. Although the couple know each other, their relationship has not been tested outside the bubble. When Jenny left her marriage and moved in with her boyfriend, it was not quite what she expected: 'For the first time, I had to face up to his flaws. I'd sort of known that he was not a reader. His shelves were full of DVDs and a collection of sci-fi novels based on a TV series, but I'd not realised that he would be upset if I went up to bed early with a good book. Of course, when we'd been having an affair, and time was limited, I didn't want to do anything as mundane as reading! But actually, it's very important to me.'

This was not the only problem. 'At first it was bliss to spend Sunday morning in bed together, but I soon realised just how little we had in common. I'd have to wrack my brains to keep the conversation going. It hadn't seemed a problem before. What had we talked about? Then it hit me, we'd always been worrying about "our situation" or planning our next time together.' Jenny had known all this information before but the adrenaline rush of the affair had stopped her from taking it on board.

When someone leaves their partner to pursue their new love, expectations are through the roof. The third party is a 'soul partner' and the relationship is 'perfect'. Nothing less is acceptable. After all, the person having the affair has given up everything. Under even the best circumstances, this is a lot to ask. With guilt, shame and the family's disappointment thrown into the mixture, rows and upsets are almost guaranteed.

'Slowly, I realised that I'd made a huge mistake. Emily was wonderful but she was also a bit of a princess,' explained Mike, forty-three, who left his partner of fifteen years for his mistress. 'On her birthday, I produced a pile of presents which she quickly unwrapped and then there was an ominous silence. "Where is my main present?" she asked. She had opened it about four presents back.'

Mike started to re-evaluate his relationship with his wife, Kate. 'We had our ups and downs, but I never felt that I had to keep proving my love or that Kate measured it in the quality of the restaurants, hotels or places I took her to. We could have just as much pleasure from sitting outside a country pub on a sunny afternoon and watching the world go past.' While he had been under the influence of affair love, he had seen Emily only in white tones and Kate in black ones. Once the adrenaline rush had worn off, he realised the world was more nuanced. Three months later, Mike left Emily and he and Kate started counselling.

At this point, I should make a confession myself. When I was twenty-three, I had an affair and left the person that I had been living with. (Looking back, I should have had the courage to face our problems rather than run away into an affair, but I was young and inexperienced.) I will never forget the evening I introduced my new lover to my friends; everybody was perfectly civil but there was a frostiness in the air. It was not that my friends were particularly judgemental about the affair but they did not like my lover. Looking through their eyes, I saw all sorts of things that I didn't like, either. I ended the relationship shortly afterwards.

Normally, when a couple start to court, friends and family provide an important vetting service. Someone will say: 'She's an attractive girl but she's very possessive' or 'Did you see the way he didn't want just to split the bill and haggled over who ate what?' This allows us to step back and weigh up whether these things are important to us or not and make a considered judgement. By contrast, affair love develops in secret away from these checks and balances.

To sum up the differences:

Affair love	Married love
Bubble world	Real world
Private	Public
Untested	Tested
Black-and-white	Complex
No established roots	Deep roots
Adrenaline-fuelled	Settled routines
Glamorous	Domestic
Obsessive	Generous
Generally child-free	Children
No responsibilities	Family

There are advantages and disadvantages to all these qualities, but it is clear that affair love will eventually burn itself out. In very few cases is this translated into married love. Annette Lawson, a sociologist from Brunel University, conducted research into adultery in the eighties and found that only 10 per cent of people who left their partner ended up marrying the person with whom they had the affair. In my research, only 1 per cent were leaving their marriage for the affair partner. Even with this minority, there is not necessarily a happy ending. Shirley Glass, PhD (whose research, *Not Just Friends*, was published by the Free Press, 2004), reports that 75 per cent of unfaithful individuals who married their affair partner ended up getting divorced.

How to fight affair love

It is one thing to discover that your partner has been having an affair, but wants to save your relationship, and quite another to learn that she or he is leaving you for the third party. For many people, this is the end of their marriage; others want to fight on. If you fall into the latter category, you have chosen a tough path but there are still grounds for optimism. Here are five strategies to help increase the chances of getting your partner back:

1. *Let your partner leave*. Normally, I do not recommend separation – as this tends to make it harder to work on the issues in the relationship – but this is the exception. I have counselled couples where they have decided to stay under the same roof and live 'separate lives' but the jealousy soon becomes impossible and all the remaining goodwill is squandered on arguments about laundry, groceries and bills.

2. *Concentrate on today*. Try and focus on the next seven days. Attempting to make plans further into the future is impossible and increases the risk of being overwhelmed with 'What if?' and 'How will I cope?' questions. Looking backwards is equally destructive and likely to provoke either self-flagellation or depressive thoughts. Having said that, living in the present is hard. So be gentle with yourself if you slip up.

3. *Accept all invitations*. Staying at home and moping is good neither for your self-esteem or your chances of renewing your relationship. What is more appealing: someone who has an interesting and varied social life or someone complaining about 'poor me'?

4. *Reassess after six months.* Travel optimistically but do not fight past the point of all reasonable hope.

5. *Make certain that you are taking your partner back for the right reasons.* There is a big difference between your partner getting fed up with her or his new lover and making a firm commitment to work on your relationship again. At this point, it is easy to put doubts to one side and believe in 'happily ever after'. However, there is a lot of repair work to do and your relationship needs to move through the rest of the seven steps before reaching recovery.

Torn between two lovers

If the last scenario was difficult, this one is even more painful. The affair might be out in the open but the deceiver cannot decide where his or her future lies. On the one hand, there is a partner who wants to save the marriage and normally children, too. There is also a shared history, property and probably an 'okay' relationship. On the other, there is a new, exciting partner and the lure of the unknown. Over the duration of the affair, a bond has been forged between the deceiver and the third party which goes deeper than good sex. The person trapped in the middle of the affair triangle is aware that both their partner and their lover are hurting. He or she feels pulled first one way and then the other but is unable to find a way forward.

'I don't know which way to turn,' moaned Simon, forty-five, 'I am very drawn to my lover and fantasise about how life would be together. However, I know my wife wants us to stay together. It was our wedding anniversary the other day and we decided not to exchange presents. However, she let herself into my car and left a red rose on the dashboard. It was a really nice gesture and my heart soared.' Simon was trying to balance a three-year affair – which had fed him both intellectually and sexually – and a twenty-year marriage with three children in their teens. He had felt unfulfilled for several years and that his life had been corralled by other people's expectations. What should he do?

Although I listened sympathetically, I was not really in the position to help. Counselling is not a good forum for making this sort of decision. In the past, when I first qualified, I would listen while someone went through all the pros and cons of staying and going. It was agony. All I achieved was to deepen the confusion and help my client to better understand being stuck.

A few weeks later, Simon contacted me again. He had decided to work on his marriage and I arranged a session for both him and his wife, Celia. However, we could not start repairing their relationship because the affair had not really ended. He might not have seen or had sexual relations with the other woman, but they spoke on the phone several times a day. 'I told her that I'm trying to save my marriage,' explained Simon. 'She got terribly upset and I sort of backtracked a bit.' 'So you haven't told her it's over?' asked Celia. 'Not in so many words,' Simon replied.

Celia was particularly upset that he had disappeared during a family holiday abroad. When she finally found him, he was in a quiet corner talking to the other woman on his mobile. 'She has broken her arm and she's been really down. I feel responsible and I can't just abandon her like that,' said Simon. 'She has nobody else beyond me.' At this point, Celia broke in: 'She has a husband.'

As Simon and Celia argued, it became clear that both of them were torn in two – but in different ways. Simon wanted to work on his marriage and still keep contact with the other woman: 'My plan is to wean her off me gradually.' He had talked to a friend of theirs who had let her husband continue to see the other woman (who had eventually found another lover) and they were still happily together.

Meanwhile, Celia was equally torn and vacillating first one way and then the other: 'I know that I should think Simon's suggestion over.' She stopped for a second. 'How would it work? Would it involve you seeing her? You might sleep with her again.' Simon agreed that might happen. Celia gave him a dark look and I asked what it meant. 'I couldn't bear that.' Celia sunk further into her chair and sighed. 'I wish I could be stronger, because if Simon could get her out of his system . . .' Her voice trailed away. She definitely wanted to save her marriage but at what cost? If this impasse was not painful enough, each partner's indecision and lack of clarity was feeding into the other's. Almost three months after the discovery of the affair, it seemed that they were no further forward.

If this is your dilemma, how do you break the deadlock? If you are the deceived, it might seem that you will never reach the Hope stage. However, there is something that you can do. Instead of waiting for your partner to make his or her decision, you can look at your own indecisiveness. Your partner might not know what he or she wants, but you need to be clear about what is acceptable and unacceptable behaviour.

The next counselling session with Celia and Simon was completely different because Celia had done just that: 'I could not live with the other woman in my house, and that's how it felt because she could text or phone at any time. If he wanted to continue to speak to her; he should not live with me and the children. So I asked him to move out.' This had concentrated Simon's mind. 'I missed the kids so much. It was horrible.' He tried to negotiate returning at the weekends but Celia was firm: he could not sleep at home. As Celia had stopped vacillating, Simon began to focus on the reality of his 'weaning' strategy: 'How can I support her through the pain of splitting up, when I'm the person who is causing the pain in the first place?' He had resolved to be honest with the other woman and end the affair. 'I guess she suspects what I'm going to say and that's making it worse.'

There were several reasons for this positive outcome. Celia had decided what she could live with and what she could not. Her decision had not been made in anger nor as a threat, and therefore she was able to stick to it. In addition, Celia had contained the crisis into a small and manageable time frame. She asked Simon to leave 'for the time being' and 'until you make your mind up'. This had also left the door open for him to return.

There is a second tool for breaking the deadlock and this is to stop 'second-guessing' your partner. When Emma's husband left their four-year marriage and set up home with his girlfriend, she spent a lot of energy reading his behaviour for positive and negative signs: 'He would take her to a place where a close friend bartended and I frequented often. He also took her to his brother's wedding only two weeks after I found out about the affair.' Emma was certain that he had deliberately set out to 'humiliate' her.

Conversely, when he sent her four emails saying 'sorry that he hurt me, to call him whenever at his new cell phone number and say hi to baby bird [that he gave me as a Valentine's present]', she saw this as a desire to get back together again. Stepping back from the situation, there are many alternative interpretations to her husband's behaviour: he could have gone to the wedding for the free booze rather than to humiliate her. He could have sent the emails to assuage his guilt about the affair rather than to start again. With my therapist hat on, I see a man who is trying to keep both of his options open and will, in all probability, make both women unhappy. However, it is pointless trying to second-guess. There are multiple possible interpretations for our partner's behaviour and our responses are open to multiple interpretations, too. There is supposition on top of supposition and the ground is shifting so much that it is impossible to make any progress.

If this sounds all too familiar, you can break out of second-guessing by being very clear about your motivation and asking for a similar courtesy from your partner. Returning to Emma and her husband's emails, she should have asked: 'Why have you contacted me?' This response would have invited an answer and clarification, while playing along provided only confusion and helped her fall deeper in love. She was thinking of calling and meeting up – even though he was still living with the other woman – but this would have just perpetuated the triangle. 'I saw him, by chance, in town and he looked so miserable and different from the smiley, clean, happy guy he was with me,' she explained. It was hard but Emma needed to step back and wait until her husband had made his long-term decision.

For the Discovered: Hope

- Everything is not lost. The two of you can be a couple again.

- However, you need to make a clean break with your former lover and help your partner feel safe again.

- Although you might be concerned for the welfare of your former lover, trying to 'keep in touch' or 'be friends' sends the wrong signal and makes your partner feel anxious and unloved. It will also prolong mourning for your affair and make recovery harder for everyone.

- If a clean break is not possible – because the third party was a work colleague – make certain contact is kept to a minimum and on a strictly business footing. This means not asking after her mother or his children or sharing bits of office gossip.

- Volunteer information about any fresh, unavoidable contact with the third party – show emails or texts (however inconsequential) and warn in advance about shared work projects (even if there will be other people in the room). This is an opportunity to prove that you are trustworthy.

- Our natural inclination is to enjoy the Hope stage and do everything to stay in calm waters. Although opening up to your partner and answering questions about the affair might seem painful or even destructive, this is actually another chance to offer proof that you want your relationship to succeed. Ultimately, truthfulness and full disclosure will prolong hope.

- Bizarre as it might seem, your partner's need to reconstruct your affair is also part of the healing process. The facts – however unwholesome – are better than his or her fevered imaginings. For example, when Julie, thirty-one, discovered her partner had cheated with someone he met at her best friend's wedding, she wanted to know everything – even the positions used in bed: 'However, the more I dug the less interesting the whole thing sounded. The more he talked about it the less he could believe that he did it.'

- You can help your partner feel safe again by being accountable for your whereabouts and phoning if you are held up. If your affair is tied up with some particular behaviour – for example, being on the computer, playing tennis or business trips – volunteer to cut-down or temporarily stop these activities.

- If you are feeling ambivalent about staying, or you're missing your ex, do not keep this to yourself – especially if your partner asks, 'What's the matter?' Being truthful rebuilds communication between the two of you and stops your feelings from festering.

- It is normal to need time to mourn and let go of your affair partner. These feelings do not necessarily mean that you have made the wrong decision.

- Do not be surprised if your mood swings from optimism to despair – it is common after a trauma. Over the next few weeks, the violent changes will begin to lessen – especially if you follow the clean break and 'safety-first' policy.

New skill: Finding a positive out of a negative

Before looking in detail at this skill, I have a few examples of it in action. The first comes from a newspaper. One morning, when John Aherne from Edinburgh looked out of the window into his front garden, something was missing: 'We had this big ornamental lion which has been in our family for more than a hundred years. My grandmother sat on it, my mother sat on it, I sat on it as did my children and my grandchildren.' It would be easy to be angry but John tried to take it with good grace. 'At least the thieves were polite and closed the gate behind them.'

The second example comes from my casebook. Eleanor was going through a tough time. Her much-loved father had died after a long illness and her marriage was disintegrating. She did not even feel capable of looking after her two small children and had let her husband have custody. Losing her driving licence, after failing a breathalyser test, could have been the final straw. However, Eleanor decided to see the positive: 'It was terribly inconvenient having to take buses everywhere but I really think someone was looking out for me. If I hadn't been stopped by the police, I would have probably gone completely out of control and ended up crashing and hurting myself, someone else, or who knows what else.'

In even the worst scenarios, people have found unlikely positives from a negative. One of my clients spoke about her father's death and her mother's attempt to find humour out of the bleakest of occasions: 'At least it's finally settled the long-standing dispute about where to put the piano.'

What these stories share is a sense of loss and, even if your partner is fully committed to staying and fighting for your relationship, it still feels like a bereavement. You are mourning the loss of your image of your partner as someone who would not be deliberately cruel and also that his or her unfaithfulness has robbed the meaning from a chunk of your life. However, these stories also show that something positive can be retrieved from even the bleakest moments. Ultimately what is important is not the trials and tribulations of life but how we interpret our experiences and the significance we attach to them. To help you achieve this new skill of finding a positive out of a negative, see 'Turning lemons into lemonade' in the exercise section below.

Summary

- Hope is the most fleeting of the seven stages of recovery and it is normal to have down days.
- Your recovery will be directly linked to the behaviour of your partner. The transition from perpetrator of the hurt to healer is difficult, but it is helped by answering questions after the affair and being transparent about movements, feelings and any contact with the third party.
- Although affairs tend to be very passionate, they take place in an isolated bubble and, when exposed to reality, will often implode.
- After wobbly moments, when you are angry with your partner, it is important to follow up with reassurance: this is a short-term reaction and your long-term ambition is still to heal the relationship.
- Ultimately, one of the best ways to recover from infidelity is to find meaning out of your pain and distress. It is an opportunity for new insights and new behaviour. This mindset will both prolong the Hope stage and help you find a way back after some fresh revelation undermines your confidence.

Exercises

Building in treats

In the early stages of recovery, it is all angst and long discussions. These are necessary but they are also exhausting. So it is good to build a little fun into your life too.

- A relationship is a living thing and like all living things needs feeding to thrive. So set aside a block of two hours once a week to share a pleasurable experience together.
- It is best to make this an activity – where there are things to talk about beyond the relationship – rather than just going out for a meal together. I would also avoid alcohol, too. Some examples could include: going to an art gallery, rummaging through junk and charity shops together, going bowling, watching a movie or going for a walk at some local beauty spot.
- If you feel safer taking the children or friends, so be it, but I would recommend, over time, trying to cut back the family and group outings and to concentrate on quality time as a couple.
- To ensure that these treats are a reality rather than an aspiration, it is important to plan ahead and defend the time against other demands. (Watch how easily your treats can be encroached upon, this is how your relationship became stale beforehand.)
- Be creative. If you have young children and it is not easy to get babysitters, arrange for them to have tea with a friend and leave work early so that you slot in your treat before their bedtime. Remember, a treat only needs to be two hours – but don't stint yourself and slice time off the end.
- The three keys to a great treat are fun, delight and playfulness.

Turning lemons into lemonade

Lemons taste sharp and bitter – however, they can be turned into something delicious and refreshing like lemonade. Here are some suggestions of how to transform your recent experiences into something sweeter:

- Look back over your life and choose three events which were painful at the time. For example, failing an exam, moving schools, the birth of a younger sibling, a bereavement or your parent's divorce. Think about how you felt at the time, allow yourself to feel the full range of feelings associated with the event, remember how you imagined life would be. Next, compare the reality with what happened. How good were you at predicting the amount and the duration of the pain? What did you learn? What positives flowed directly from this time? (Taking a personal example: when my first partner died in 1997, I started keeping a diary to make sense of my feelings and from that flowed a career in writing.)
- Look back into history to discover the positives that have sprung out of terrible events. For example the United Nations was founded in 1945 after World War II to provide a platform for countries to solve their differences. It has also spawned bodies like the World Health Organization and the United Nations Children's Fund. Can you name three national or international events that seemed purely a disaster and find the positives that were a direct result of them?
- Look back over the past weeks and months since the discovery of your partner's infidelity. What have you learnt about yourself? In what ways have you surprised yourself? What have you learnt about your partner since the discovery? How have both of you changed?

Letting go of blame

Our society is quick to apportion blame – after all, it is an important part of our legal system – and when discussing infidelity people often use phrases like 'innocent' and 'guilty' parties. Unfortunately, in relationships blame heats up emotion, builds up anger and prevents problem-solving. This is one of the main reasons why I do not use these terms. In nearly all the cases where couples are stuck and cannot reach hope, they have become trapped in an endless cycle of blaming, attacking and defending. So this exercise accepts that we often need to blame but recognises that it is self-defeating, and helps you climb out of the trap.

1. Get a large piece of paper and draw lines to divide it into four.
2. Into the first quarter write your name and into the second write your partner's name. The third party's name goes into the third quarter and into the final quarter put the names of anybody you blame for encouraging, facilitating or not warning you of the affair. If there is nobody who fits this description, leave it blank.
3. Under each name make a list of all the things you blame that person for. For example, for yourself: 'How could I be so blind?', or for the third person, 'She stole him', or 'He took advantage'. Keep going until you have put down everything.
4. Look at the lists again. Is there something that you have missed off? However stupid it may seem, it is better out of your head and on paper.
5. Read the lists for a final time and write down some of the counter arguments: 'Nobody can steal another person. He had legs and made his own choice' or 'I wanted to believe in the best of her.'
6. Finally, make a commitment to yourself to let go of blame and perform a small ceremony of destruction for your sheet of blame – by setting fire to it, shredding it or tearing it up.

7. Next time you find your brain beginning to channel you down the same path, remind yourself: 'I have let go of blame', and picture the paper being destroyed again.

The trust continuum

At halfway through the seven stages from discovery to recovery, it is useful to take stock and consider the central issue of trust. Although, after an affair, many people see trust in black-and-white terms: either you trust someone or you do not. It is more helpful to think of trust as a continuum, rather than as an on-off switch. So draw the following scale:

No trust ◄───────────────────────────► Complete trust

1. Where would you put yourself on this scale at the moment?
2. How far towards the 'Complete trust' end have you moved in the last few weeks?
3. Write down all the areas in which you still trust your partner. (For example, to collect the children from school, to prepare supper, to pay the car tax, to pay his or her salary into the joint account, to buy a card for your mother's birthday.)
4. Keep going and write more things down.
5. Add the specific areas where you do not trust your partner. This will provide some focus for planning your 'safety-first' living.
6. However, the main aim of this exercise is to demonstrate how even at this tentative stage, your partner is more trustworthy than you imagined.

Checkpoint

Three key points for enjoying Stage Four: Hope

1. Concentrate on living in the present tense. Harking back to a golden past will make you depressed. Trying to imagine the future will make you anxious.
2. Think about what you need for coping day-to-day, and don't be afraid to ask for it.
3. Comparing yourself with the affair partner is a blind alley.

Stage Five:
Attempted Normality

RECOVERY

Attempted Normality

Hope

Decision Time

Intense Questioning

Shock and Disbelief

DISCOVERY

Many people, when they reach Stage Five, let out a big sigh of relief. They think the drama of the affair is behind them: their partner has decided to either 'work on the relationship' or 'give it another try'. After the drama, pain and naked passion of the past weeks and months, everything seems normal. However, it is all on the surface. I've called this stage 'Attempted Normality' because couples desperately want their lives back in the old familiar patterns but there is no trust, no real understanding of what happened and no sense of how to get from here to the future – beyond a general desire to 'try harder'. In effect, they have not engaged with the three fundamental beliefs that underpin our lives (introduced in the first chapter), which are ruptured by the discovery of an affair:

1. The world is benevolent. (Good things happen to good people.)
2. The world is meaningful. (There is a plan and things happen for a reason.)
3. I am worthy. (Therefore good things will happen to me.)

In effect, these couples fear that the world is malevolent. (Terrible things happen to people who are trying their best.) The world is meaningless. (Why did it happen to me?) I feel worthless. (If I was truly loved, none of this would have happened.)

So my advice when you reach Stage Five is to enjoy your snatched moments of normality. You deserve a rest on this long and arduous journey, but do not be surprised when difficult emotions disturb your Attempted Normality or life seems strangely flat and grey. In many ways, this step is rather like the months before discovering your partner's affair. On the one hand, everything feels normal, but on the other, there is this worrying 'can't quite put my finger on it' sensation. A vital piece of the jigsaw is missing but you are not certain what. The last time you experienced something similar you were about to discover that your partner had been cheating. Therefore, it is not surprising that many Discoverers leap to the conclusion that the affair has started up again or, in fact, never finished. Sometimes, this can be true.

However, in the majority of the cases that I counsel, something entirely different is happening. Deep down, people know that the journey is not over. There is more learning needed to reach recovery, to re-establish a sense of the world as benevolent and to trust again. In effect, this is the missing piece of the jigsaw and will be the central theme of the next two chapters. But first, I want to look further at your disquiet and the fear that all your progress is about to unravel. These feelings are so strong – almost primeval – that my rational explanations will probably not be enough to soothe them. Worse still, these feelings can actually derail the healing process. So what's going on?

Aftershock

In geology, the first earthquake is normally the worst but it is common for smaller aftershocks to follow. These are particularly dangerous because they are unpredictable and can collapse buildings that have already been damaged by the main shock. In many ways, the discovery of an affair is like an earthquake in a relationship. The aftershock normally comes in the lull after the drama of assessing the damage and rescuing the marriage, and when everything appears to be returning to normal. As with a real earthquake, relationship aftershocks undermine unstable structures – in this case truces or pacts to 'try harder' and preliminary attempts to rebuild trust. So what causes aftershocks?

In some cases, it is very straightforward. The Discoverer has been told or uncovered something about the affair, or the third party is back on the scene in some way. More often, the origin of the aftershock is harder to pin down and seems to come out of nowhere. Whatever the cause, these feelings are incredibly uncomfortable. Most people just want them to go away, so they employ *three* different strategies: suppression, obsession and hyper-vigilance.

Suppression

Around this time in counselling, my clients often arrive with long faces. There's no need to ask how their week has gone, it is written on their faces. Normally, the Discoverer will confess that 'things are terrible' and the Discovered will complain, 'We've been arguing over the most stupid things.' These setbacks are particularly worrying for my clients because on the surface everything seemed to be going so well. In reality, one or both partners have been suppressing their feelings and, in particular, their anxiety or guilt.

A good example are Oliver and Samantha, in their early thirties with two primary-school-aged children. Five months previously, Oliver had several sexual encounters with one of Samantha's friends. His first reaction had been to minimise the affair: 'It didn't mean that much' and 'I think you're overreacting.' These are typical suppressions. However, during counselling, he had opened up and admitted to Samantha and himself that he had betrayed his wife, spoilt her friendship and made it impossible for his children to see their old playmates again. However, during Attempted Normality, he began to shut down again. 'I don't see the point of bringing this up over and over again. I feel guilty enough as it is. It just upsets Samantha and I can't see the point.'

Again these are typical comments from someone using suppression to cope with difficult emotions. The situation had become worse because Samantha had also begun to suppress her feelings too: 'I don't want to keep going on and on at Oliver.' However, she still had a long way to go before she could reach recovery.

When there is a lot of suppression, and the feelings are bubbling away under the surface, it only takes something minor – like a tone of voice – to set off a nasty argument. Small issues can trigger black moods and sometimes even days of misery. When a couple finally start talking again they cannot understand how and why the row started. Worse still, they think, 'If we can't get on over little things, how on earth are we going to solve the big ones?'

To explain what's happening, I have broken down one of Samantha and Oliver's arguments. At ten o'clock one Saturday morning, Oliver was about to switch on the family computer, answer his emails and do his banking. Samantha brought him a coffee and they took a break from their morning duties on the patio together. After a few moments of strained silence, she drained her cup and decided to cut the grass. He was annoyed, because it was his job and he tried to placate her by getting out the strimmer to do the edges of the grass. This strategy failed. They spent the next twenty-four hours ignoring each other, being overly polite or sniping. Does this sound familiar? How could something so normal go so wrong? Here is what was said at the time and I've also added in what was happening under the surface.

Samantha: 'Let's go and have our coffee in the garden.' **What she really meant:** *I need to talk about the affair but I don't want to do it in front of the children.*

Oliver: 'Okay.' Instead of switching on the computer, he picks up his laptop and takes it outside on to the patio. **What he is communicating with this body language:** *I've got a lot of things to do. Let's not spoil the weekend by raking over old territory.*

They go outside and sit in silence for a while.

Samantha is thinking: *Here's your chance to talk about the affair, our progress so far, counselling, how to move forward. Anything. Don't just sit there.*

Oliver has his laptop on his knees but he has not switched it on. **What he is communicating with this body language:** *I'm not keen on this* [the laptop is like a barrier between them] *but if you must,* *go ahead. I've shown that I'm willing to listen because I have not switched the computer on.*

The silence builds.

Samantha is thinking: *Why is it always me who has to do all the work? He goes off and has an affair but it's me who has to pick up the pieces.* She gives him a daggers look. **What she is communicating with this body language:** *Put away the laptop.*

Oliver knows that she is angry about the laptop but does nothing. *It was she who wanted to talk about the bloody affair and now she's just sitting there. I knew this was a bad idea – all we do is go over the same old ground.*

Samantha drains her coffee cup. **What she is communicating with this body language:** *So I'm not going to have your undivided attention and you're not going to talk. Have it your own way. See if I care.*

She goes off and prepares to cut the lawn. **What she is thinking:** *I've got better things to do than sit around – unlike you.* [After all, cutting the lawn is his job.] **What she is communicating with this body language:** *I can manage without you.*

Oliver tries to stop her: 'I was just about to get round to that.' **What he is thinking:** *Give me a chance.*

She ignores his pleas. **What she is communicating with this body language:** *I'm punishing you for making me miserable, for not talking when I needed you to and for having the affair in the first place.*

Oliver gets out the strimmer. **What he is communicating with this body language:** *I'm sorry. Let me cut the grass. At least let me help you.*

They angrily garden together. **What she is communicating with this body language:** *After how you've treated me, you can't buy me off with a pathetic little gesture like that.* **What he is communicating with this body language:** *Can't you see I'm trying?*

They put away the gardening equipment. **What she is thinking:** *How can we move forward if he refuses to talk. What's the point?* **What he is thinking:** *I can't do anything right. What's the point?*

Less than a dozen words have been spoken out loud, but a furious row has been conducted below the surface. Interestingly, they both ended up feeling the same despair. However, rather than being able to reach out to each other, they retreated into their own separate routines. Nothing was resolved, even when they started to talk the next morning. When I reconstructed the silent row in the counselling room, Oliver and Samantha were actually very good at reading each other's body language but were powerless to stop the row escalating. This is because:

- Body language is open to misinterpretation.
- We are often not aware of all the layers of meaning in even our own body language.
- Body language is easy to dispute. Even if one person says, 'You are looking hostile', the other can easily claim, 'There's nothing wrong with me'.

In the final part of this exercise, I asked Samantha and Oliver to have the same conversation but bring the subtext (the body language and unspoken communication) up to the surface. This is what happened:

Samantha: 'There are a couple of things that are really getting me down and this would be a good opportunity to talk.'

Oliver: 'Is this really such a good time? The kids are around and I don't want to spoil their day with a row. Couldn't we talk about it later?'

Samantha: 'If you really mean it.'

Oliver: 'Yes. After the children are in bed.'

Samantha: 'Okay.'

In this way, Samantha and Oliver not only expressed themselves more clearly but were also finally able to negotiate. They also learnt that the small things had been connected to larger issues, but without this understanding they could neither co-operate on the gardening nor reconcile their different approaches to resolving the adultery.

If you or your partner have been suppressing feelings or worries, use the making-up phase after a row to delve behind the immediate trigger point to discuss underlying tensions.

Obsession

This aftershock is the polar opposite of suppression. Instead of trying to forget, someone using this coping mechanism will go over the affair again and again, looking for the 'killer' piece of information that will help make sense of their pain. Sometimes this is because the Discovered has held details back (either out of supposed kindness or to protect themselves) or has been so guarded that it is difficult to reconstruct the affair. If this sounds familiar, re-read 'How to tackle your partner' and 'Improve your communication style' in Stage One: Shock and Disbelief.

However, a more common reason for obsession during Attempted Normality is that the Discoverer is dealing with flashbacks. These can be triggered by something specific – like infidelity on a soap opera, a celebrity story in the newspapers or the Discovered being late home – but they frequently come out of nowhere. Flashbacks are involuntary, vivid images which bring back all the most traumatic moments of betrayal. 'I'd be walking upstairs to put away the laundry and suddenly, out of nowhere, I'd be gripped by the idea that she had walked up these stairs and I'd feel humiliated all over again,' explained Imogen, thirty-five. 'The pictures were so intense that I'd want to tear up the carpet or burn the bed where he and she had copulated together.' There are two common responses to these flashbacks: flooding and over-thinking.

Flooding

The emotions are so intense and overwhelming that the Discoverer has to get rid of them. There seems only one solution: to pour them all out on the Discovered. After all, the Discoverer will later reason: it's good to express my feelings. This is true, but only up to a point. When someone is flooded, all rational thought is swept away, and the emotions come out in one unthinking torrent.

'I'd call Gabriel terrible names and tell him horrible things – like I would never forgive him – which actually weren't true,' explained Imogen. 'But my anger would just build and build and out would come this stuff that I didn't actually feel. I knew things were getting better but once on my rant there was no stopping me.'

Rather than being a healing release – which can happen if someone has been suppressing their feelings – these outpourings pump up the anger and make things worse. In Gabriel and Imogen's case, the flooding was particularly harmful because Gabriel became flooded too. 'I would think "She's right, you're a complete and utter bastard, how could you have been so selfish?" and I'd be overwhelmed with guilt and self-hatred,' said Gabriel, 'and I'd forget all the progress that we'd made.' At least in this case, the lines of communication remained open. Normally, when the Discoverer rants, the Discovered will suppress his or her feelings and try to contain an out-of-control situation. This only increases the Discoverer's tendency to flood. So what can be done?

If you have a tendency to flood, the first job is to calm your thoughts. In this way, you will not be sucked downwards into this self-defeating and destructive spiral. With Imogen, I asked her to prepare a positive current image to counterbalance the negative flashback. 'I could remember this day out by the seaside and how he'd booked a table at a restaurant that I'd read about in the paper,' said Imogen. 'It really showed how much he was thinking and listening to me and we had a wonderful day together.'

The next week, Imogen and Gabriel felt more positive: 'I had a flashback but I immediately substituted it for the moment he squeezed my hand in the restaurant – that and the taste of their crayfish linguine.' It is important to make the positive picture as detailed as possible, so stay in the moment and think about all your senses: tastes, smells and sounds as well as sights. However, Imogen had not completely ignored her feelings. In the evening, she told Gabriel that she'd had a difficult day and they had a cuddle on the sofa. 'I felt reassured that he did love me and was trying to make things better and actually he didn't need to hear all the stuff going on in my head.' (There is more about this in the exercise 'Getting on the same page'.) Other ways of combating flooding include:

- *Putting up your mental STOP sign and rescheduling the thoughts for later in the day.* Often, when the time comes, there will be nothing to consider or just some small thing that needs calmly discussing.
- *Riding the wave.* Tell yourself, this is a natural response to stress and although it will be painful, I will cope and come out the other side. Afterwards, read positive self-help books or go for a run and burn off some of the worry.
- *Learn to self-soothe.* Instead of using your partner or friends (who can unthinkingly build up your sense of being the injured party) to take the edge of your feelings, learn to calm yourself down. This could be pampering yourself, doing something that you're good at (which rebuilds your self-worth) or losing yourself in an engrossing hobby.

- *Keep a journal and pour out all your feelings to yourself.* Later, you can read through and pick out any essentials that need to be communicated to your partner. It is also useful to go back over the journal and see how much progress has been made.

Over-thinking

The second kind of obsession is the flip side of the first. While flooding is a very emotional response, over-thinking is a very rational one. From childhood, we have been trained to 'think it through', explore all the options and come to a calm, considered decision. Certainly, it is useful for mathematical problems, the causes of the Hundred Years War and the first stages after discovering an affair. However, there is a very fine line between analysing and dwelling on a problem, and, by Stage Five, thinking about the problem is not necessarily an asset. In fact, it can easily tip into being destructive.

Charlotte, thirty-five, had always considered her ability to reason with a problem as an asset. When she discovered that her husband had been cheating with one of her best friends, she found out the facts and quickly came to the conclusion that she should tell her friend's husband. She had no problems deciding the right formula and dispatched the task as swiftly and with as much compassion as possible. As her friend had done much of the running, her husband, Michael, was truly sorry and because the adultery had happened on only a handful of occasions, Charlotte decided to give her marriage another try. She researched her options for counselling and contacted Relate.

However, by the couple's fourth session, she was beginning to become more and more depressed. She wanted to know *why* he had been unfaithful. What was Michael's reaction? 'He tries to be patient, but he soon gets angry.' 'But you keep asking questions that I can't answer. I'm sorry, but I can't tell you why I did it.' Michael's best guess was that he and Charlotte were 'taking each other for granted'. However, Charlotte could not believe that he could jeopardise their marriage and the happiness of their children on such a flimsy pretext. 'What more do you want? I don't know!' Michael flat-walled. The couple lapsed into gloomy silence.

'What are you trying to achieve from these questions?' I asked Charlotte. As I guessed, she was looking for more than answers. 'Reassurance that everything will be okay,' she explained. 'Except, we end up arguing and I feel worse but asking questions is the only way to get things out of my head.' What else could she do? Charlotte thought for a moment: 'Ask him for a cuddle and then tell him about my fears.' During the next week, she did indeed try this approach and on several occasions Michael gave her a hug without her asking. The week went much better and the couple made big strides towards recovery.

If this sounds familiar, you are probably not just looking for reassurance. Under all the turmoil, there are often one or two simple questions or problems, but they are lost as all the hurt is pumped up by over-thinking. This is why I recommend writing down your thoughts. No matter how small or stupid, put it down on paper and keep going. It is almost as if you are taking dictation; don't question, just write it down until there is nothing left in your head. Here is what Charlotte wrote down when the other woman dropped off her older child at the school where Charlotte works:

Stomach turns.
I can't believe she kissed him.
I can't believe she went behind my back.
I'll never get over this.
All the planning that went into courting him.
How dare she show her face.
I can't believe that she thinks her life will carry on as before.
Should I talk to her?

As I expected, underneath all the over-thinking, there was *one* serious question and it needed an answer. Should I talk to her? This is Charlotte's answer: *Yes, but I don't want to make a scene when the children are around. What would it really achieve?*

Later, when the other woman brought her younger child to look around the classroom where Charlotte was a teaching assistant, she wrote:

Shock.
Can't believe she's going to carry on regardless.
She could easily send the child to another local school.
I'm always going to get ambushed by this woman.
Panic.
Get a grip on yourself.
Should I tell the Head Teacher?

This was her answer to the question about telling the Head: *I don't know.*
Charlotte learnt some important lessons from this exercise:

- When everything was down on paper, she was surprised that there were fewer items than expected.
- With the thoughts no longer circling her mind but down on paper, she could test their accuracy. For example, she amended 'I'll never get over this' to the more accurate: 'At the moment, I feel like I will never get over this.' Although this is only a small difference, it makes the problem more contained and more soluble.
- She could also dispute facts: 'I'm always going to get ambushed.' Obviously she will not always be ambushed. One day the child will grow up and leave school. Other words that suggest exaggeration are: 'never', 'forever', 'must' and 'should'. (To challenge the last two words, ask yourself: who says you must or should? Could it be that you can choose to do something rather than be compelled? Another small but significant change.)
- Charlotte also realised that she did own a STOP signal and could train herself not to become obsessive. In this case, it was because she had a class of small children who needed her attention and 'got a grip'. However, she could also use this trick at home too.

- Finally, she learnt that she did not necessarily have to answer her questions immediately. She could take them home and discuss them with Michael. (On whether to confide in the Head Teacher or not, they decided to let things ride for a while and later reassess whether Charlotte was still having problems.) 'After our discussions, I felt that we were a team working together again,' Charlotte fed back into the next counselling session.

Hyper-vigilance

The third kind of aftershock response often goes hand-in-hand with obsession. The Discoverer is hyper-alert, easily startled and has trouble sleeping. When the telephone rings, the Discoverer jumps – expecting more bad news. People with hyper-vigilance keep going through their partner's pockets for clues, keep checking emails, and often turn themselves into a full-time detective. I have known these partners to befriend the third party and go away on holiday with them (in order to discover more facts about the affair); to bribe security at their partner's office (in order to go through CCTV footage); and to monitor from the office car park who sat where at an inter-office meeting, involving the Discovered and the third party. Obviously these are extreme examples but many people become consumed by double-checking their partner's movements and correspondence.

So what's going on? The hyper-vigilant were so hurt by their partner's betrayal that they are determined to guard against it ever happening again. At this point in the recovery process, the only way to keep their partner faithful is either to be with them twenty-four seven or to check their every move. Every deviation from normality (however small or innocent), every fresh contact from the third party (however tangential), every new fact about the affair that is excavated (however insignificant), becomes exaggerated and is produced as evidence that the Discovered is not to be trusted.

For example, when Tony confessed to Jodie, he never expected to be fighting over 'lies' six months later. 'I agreed to have no more contact with the other woman – and I haven't,' he explained. However, he bumped into her when collecting their child from school. 'I didn't say anything. I didn't acknowledge her and didn't think any more about it. Okay, I didn't report this to Jodie because, frankly, there was nothing to report.' Unfortunately for Tony, one of Jodie's friends saw the encounter and told her. She was furious. 'How can I trust you, if you lie to me?' she complained in the couple's weekly counselling session. 'At the very worst, it was an omission,' Tony fought back, 'but nothing happened! What do you want me to do? Give a list of every woman I see when I'm not with you?' He folded his arms. 'I'm not worried about everyone, just that woman,' said Jodie.

Their argument had been going round in circles for days – but at least they were arguing. Often the issue goes underground because the more one partner becomes hyper-vigilant, the more the other becomes secretive – not to cover up any infidelity but because no one has the energy to justify every minute of their day. So how can you break this circle?

I asked Jodie and Tony to swap seats and make their partner's case. Tony explained that Jodie thought the casual contact would lead to them starting the affair again. 'No, I don't think you'd be stupid enough. But if you hadn't "omitted" to tell me how she'd given you little presents and taken you for a birthday coffee and cake – then I could have stepped in before you were sucked into an affair.' Finally, Tony understood that Jodie had been more upset by the lies (and his lack of honesty) than his being sexually unfaithful. When Jodie made Tony's case she said: 'If I'd told you I'd bumped into her, I'd have had days of grief.' Finally, Jodie understood that her reaction to any news about the other woman made it harder for Tony to be frank.

By going deeper into their underlying fears about honesty, rather than trying to prove or disprove something, they found a compromise: Tony agreed to make a full disclosure and Jodie agreed to keep a sense of proportion about what she heard. Their relationship quickly improved and they ended counselling with not only better overall communication but also a deeper love for each other.

If you are currently trapped in hyper-vigilance, here are some questions to ask yourself:

1. *How reliable is the information that I find?* It is easy to misinterpret emails and texts, as it is impossible to know if someone is being flippant or serious. Could you be pumping up your fears unnecessarily?

2. *Do I really need to know everything?* What if you uncover something that will haunt you or seriously derail your recovery? 'I found a CD containing very graphic nude images of the other woman about four months after the affair. He had forgotten about it,' said Bethany, twenty-eight. 'After seeing that, I found sex very disturbing for many months as the images kept popping into my head. Even now, I still struggle with it from time to time, and I can't bear him performing certain sexual acts on me as I know full well that the other woman enjoyed doing that with him.'

3. *How could I cut back?* Checking is addictive. The more that you uncover, the more it will pump up your suspicions and the more you will check. So try and break the cycle by distracting yourself: watch a favourite TV programme or phone a friend instead. If you cannot cut back, concentrate on understanding the modus operandi of the affair (how your partner found the time to be away and how she or he kept everything secret) rather than uncovering all the details. By knowing the 'how', you are in a better place to stop it from happening again.

4. *What alternative ways are there of self-soothing?* The idea is to find other ways, beyond worrying, to undo the knot in your stomach. I have had clients who started lap swimming (to occupy their bodies) and others who have learnt poetry by heart (to occupy their minds). What could you do?

Inquisitor versus accused

The most common pattern of dealing with the aftershock of discovery is for the person who had the affair to suppress and for their partner to obsess or be hyper-vigilant. Under these circumstances, each party will slide into totally different mind-sets that drive them further and further apart.

Accused	Inquisitor
'How can we move on if you can't forget?'	'How can I move on if you won't talk about it?'
'I've apologised a million times, what more can I do?'	'You never acknowledge how hurt I'm feeling.'
'We'll cross that bridge when we come to it.'	'I need to know what's on the other side to feel safe.'
'Can't we just move on?'	'It feels like you're blaming me for our problems.'
'I forget the details'	'You're trying to shut me out.'
'I love you, isn't that enough?'	'It's not that simple.'

To further underline how destructive a relationship becomes when a couple get stuck in the accused and inquisitor rut, here are two replies from my 'Adultery in the UK' survey.

'Naturally, she used the affair and aspects of it against me. I was besieged in a castle, except I was giving her the ammunition for the siege engines,' says Jimmy, thirty-six. 'And telling her once wasn't enough either. We had to go over and over the detail. Sometimes she would be in so much of a state that she couldn't take it in fully the first time round. So she would ask again and I'd get frustrated, she would become enraged and I just wanted to forget.'

If it sounds bad to be on the receiving end of the inquisition, the powerlessness of not knowing is equally painful. 'I thought that I'd found out most of what happened in the first few days,' says Janice, forty-two, about the four-month affair her husband had with a work colleague. 'However, six months later, I got a call from his mobile which had gone off in his pocket by accident, so I could overhear his business lunch. A divine being warning me, I think. I had asked him in a letter two days before not to have any social interaction with her, but here they were, entertaining clients together! I was so crazy by the time he spoke to me that he left his meeting and came straight home.' The whole situation was made worse because her husband was the line manager of the other woman. 'Even though he told me that it stopped the minute I found out, the thought of him talking to her every day made me sick with jealousy. After months of excuses, while first she and then he were supposed to be looking for a new job, I gave them an ultimatum: if she wasn't gone by Christmas, I would tell her husband and throw my husband out.' The other woman finally left, twenty months after discovery, but even now Janice still has questions. 'I still have lots of doubts and anxieties but cannot bring them up because it is all in the past – but life without him would be worse as we actually get along really well and we don't argue any more.'

So how do you solve the inquisitor versus accused dilemma? The best way to understand this problem is to think of two people on a see-saw. The more one person pushes down on their side, the more their partner goes up on their side. Therefore the more the inquisitor demands answers, the more defensive the accused will become. Conversely, the more the accused becomes defensive, the more the inquisitor will press for answers. Fortunately, there is an alternative:

- When there is a moment of truce, talk about the inquisitor versus accused see-saw and make a pact to find a balanced middle way.
- Acknowledge the progress that has been made in your recovery and thank your partner for the changes in his or her behaviour that have brought you to this point.
- Try and be proportionate in your anger. There is a difference between discovering some old sin (for example,

an email from when the affair was active where your partner poured out his or her heart) and a recent sin (for example, not telling you about some new contact from the third party).

- Frame your anxieties so they are focused on your relationship today, rather than on the past affair. For example, instead of 'How could you have written that to her?', change it to 'I wish you'd tell me stuff like that' or 'What could I do to make it easier for you to open up to me too?'
- Regularly tell your partner that you are committed to making the relationship better.
- Look at 'Question time' in the exercise section.

At stalemate

Sometimes, couples get stuck in the Attempted Normality stage. Both partners are reasonably civil and can co-operate on basic day-to-day issues, but sex is sporadic (or non-existent) and their love is hidden under layers of hurt and miscommunication. Normally, one half of the couple desperately wants to improve the relationship and get closer but the other is holding back for fear of being hurt again. If nothing is done, these couples will gradually slide from being stuck to becoming toxic.

William, forty-eight, had concentrated on providing for his four children so he had been too busy to notice that his wife, Patsy, was dissatisfied or, later, that she was having an affair. After the infidelity was uncovered – when William had borrowed Patsy's mobile – Patsy gave up her lover but only made half-hearted attempts to save their marriage.

The first counselling session was with William only. He was very matter of fact: 'It makes no sense to break up the family. The children are happy and I've worked hard to provide a good lifestyle – a nice home, foreign holidays, and it's not as if we don't get on.' I could understand why his wife was not falling over herself to make a go of their relationship. 'I don't think anyone ever manned the barricades for good sense and a nice lifestyle,' I told him. 'It's hardly a great rallying cry.'

William slipped from business-like into depressed and for the first time, I saw the person behind the facade. Slowly, he admitted that he found it hard to show his feelings. 'Does your wife know how you feel about her?' I asked. 'We've been together since we were twenty so she should do,' he replied. 'But have you shown her what's inside?' He shook his head.

The Greek Philosopher Aristotle (384–322 BC) laid out the fundamentals for good rhetoric – the art of being persuasive – with his Tripartite Ideal and it is still the secret of breaking out of stalemate today. Aristotle writes about using pathos (emotion), logos (argument) and ethos (character – who you are and how you behave). William, for example, had been using only logos: all the rational, practical reasons for staying together. So I helped him unpack his emotions and learn to communicate them. At this point, Patsy joined counselling but, although their relationship improved, she remained unconvinced about their long-term future. However, an argument over childcare proved the way into looking at ethos (character). 'He was even grudging about taking his sick son to the doctor's,' Patsy complained. 'I wanted to take him because it was a chance to get to know him better,' William countered. 'You had a funny way of showing it,' replied Patsy. 'I just didn't like being ordered rather than asked,' said William.

It soon became clear that William was not backing up his emotional pleas and his sound reasons for trying again with action. In other words, Patsy doubted his character. 'It's all empty words,' she finished. Once William realised his mistake, and started concentrating on ethos, the couple made giant strides and were able to progress to the next stage of recovery.

Resuming your sex life together

If you have reached Attempted Normality and not resumed full sexual relations, this is a good time to build bridges. The next stage will be challenging and a satisfying love life will provide consolation and bonding. So what stops couples making love again? Sometimes the problem is practical – still sleeping in separate beds. Sometimes it is emotional – the Discoverer is still too angry. However, most commonly, couples need to learn to be intimate again.

Dominic, thirty-five, had an affair shortly after his wife Danielle, thirty-two, had a baby. Although they had resumed intercourse after the birth, Danielle lost all desire when she discovered his Internet affair. Six months later, they had weathered the storm and although during their counselling sessions they discussed the possibility of making love again, nothing had happened yet.

'I feel that it is up to Danielle to make the first move,' said Dominic, 'she knows that I find her really attractive. But rather than pressurising, like I did before, I will wait for her.'

Danielle was confident that the desire would be there: 'I really used to enjoy our lovemaking and found it really fulfilling.' However, she lacked confidence: 'I don't want to lead him on and then reject him again.' Like many couples in this situation, they were stuck in an 'all-or-nothing syndrome'. They would avoid casual physical intimacy – like a cuddle on the sofa, having a bath together or a back rub – in case either partner saw this as an invitation to intercourse. However, without this kind of togetherness, it is impossible for desire to build and turn into lovemaking. So in our counselling session, we decided to ban intercourse for the next week. This might sound strange but knowing that cuddles can be enjoyed for their own sake will often free a couple. I knew this had been a success when Dominic and Danielle returned with smiles on their faces. They had also teased each other about not being able to go further and turned it into a game. (This is always a positive sign as good sex needs just this sense of fun and play.)

The next week, we went from cuddles – fully clothed on the sofa – to being naked together and massaging each other (but not touching sexual organs). In week three, we removed the ban and Dominic and Danielle had intercourse. 'I really felt that she desired me again,' said Dominic. 'I'd begun to think she only wanted me back as a father to the children.' Danielle was pleased at the shift too: 'Previously I'd told him that I'd forgiven him but letting myself be open with my body proved to my head that I really meant it.'

For the Discovered: Attempted Normality

- At Stage Five, it is easy to get frustrated. Despite all your best efforts, the affair still seems to hang between the two of you on a daily basis.

- Your natural inclination may be to keep your head down and try not to rock the boat. However, suppressing your feelings will only make your partner more anxious and more likely to obsess or compulsively check up.

- Try and meet your partner halfway, by continuing to be accountable but calmly explaining what kind of checking makes you particularly uncomfortable or annoyed. Could you make a trade where your partner will do 'x' for you and you will do 'y' for her or him in return?

- If you seem unable to get a fair hearing from your partner, it could be that you are relying on just one of the three ways of making a case: intellectual, emotional or character. So look back at your previous attempts: Have you been too rational? Have you kept your emotions to yourself or conversely used emotional blackmail? Does what you say about working on the relationship and what you actually do match up? How could you change?

- If this stage seems hard-going, do not be downhearted. Your partner, and maybe you, too, are still dealing with the aftershock of the discovery of your affair. This time is not a predictor for how things will be in the future.

New skill: Looking beneath the surface

Although we know that life is complicated, we much prefer to keep things simple. So when there is a problem, we tend to latch on to the most obvious explanation. If we are stressed or frightened, we are even more likely to concentrate on the surface. However, by this stage in your recovery, you should be a little more relaxed and able to look deeper and be aware of the multitude of factors that drive our behaviour.

Let's take something relatively simple, like purchasing a big-ticket item (a car or a large electrical item). List all the factors that influenced your last decision: price, performance, energy efficiency, appearance, advice from friends, opinions of experts, reputation of manufacturer, etc. Which item on your list was the most important? How did the factors reinforce or cancel each other out? Would your partner use the same criteria? How would she or he differ? Even with something that is not life-changing, like buying a freezer, there is a multitude of factors affecting our choice.

Now take a current issue between you and your partner: What factors do you think are driving her or his behaviour? Try and think of as many as possible. Any more? Next, rank them in order of importance. Finally, try and add other possible reasons. What fresh perspective does this give you? Had you originally opted for the simplest or most obvious reason?

Unfortunately, our take on what motivates our partner can, over time, be transformed from just an opinion into a hardened fact. Ultimately, it is better to be kind and give your partner the benefit of the doubt.

Summary

- After the drama of the first three stages, and the relief of the fourth, couples begin to relax and any pent-up anxiety is released.
- Many people experience an aftershock. Although the relationship seems normal again, it has not been repaired.
- There are three different common reactions to pain: suppression (withdrawing and numbing feelings); obsession

(repeatedly going over the emotions and the facts of betrayal); and being hyper-alert (forever expecting the next attack). This is a normal response to acute stress but nevertheless is very painful and risks derailing the healing process.

- The aftermath of an affair puts a lot of demands on couples' ability to communicate. The solution is always to look deeper – away from the most obvious cause of division – to face hidden worries, issues and problems. This skill will be vital for the next stage too.

Exercises

On a day-to-day basis, I'm the one who is the . . .

We all have roles to play in our life and in our relationship. Read through the following list and circle all the words that sound familiar. Next, go back and put a tick by the ones that you still feel comfortable doing and a cross beside the ones you wish to drop. For the third time round, underline all the roles or behaviours that you might like to take on in the future.

Organiser	Thinker	Bread winner	Dogsbody
Martyr	Saint	Sensible	In charge
Second Mate	Outcast	Lonely wanderer	Exhibitionist
On call	Rebel	Wet blanket	Winner
Loser	Slave driver	Slave	Seducer
Seductress	Rubbish bin	Invisible	Victim
Rescuer	Persecutor	Freak	Comic
Entertainer	Super reasonable	Put upon	Scapegoat
Critic	Fool	Confessor	Judge
Taxi driver	Pay master	Mouse	Dragon
Toughie	Softie	Wanderer	Observer
Lost soul	Voyeur	Wounded	Glutton
Ogre	Small child	Odd-one-out	Counsellor
Fixer	Preacher	Rule-maker	Know-all
Clinger	Sinner	Perfect	Passenger
Go-between	Chatterbox	Worrier	Timekeeper
Accountant	Mechanic	Doormat	Toy boy
Little girl	Quiet sufferer	Workaholic	Stupid one
Bossy boots	Prisoner	Jailer	Cleaner

If you are working through this book with your partner, you might like to photocopy this exercise so that you both do it and compare notes afterwards. How much do you agree about the division of roles? What would you both like to change?

Finally, ask yourself: how can I make my choices come true?

Getting on the same page

Infidelity raises the stakes in a relationship to such a fever pitch that it is easy to slip from being emotionally honest (and showing your feelings) to being over-emotional (feelings are so elevated that they come across in a blur of white noise). When this happens, the other partner retreats and it becomes impossible to communicate effectively. However, there is an alternative:

Part one: Stop emoting and start reporting

Emoting is the over-emotional outpouring where a few basic strong feelings build and build until they become distorted. Instead of either emoting or trying to ignore your feelings (which probably guarantees you will become over-emotional at the next trigger), start reporting your feelings to your partner. For example: 'I found that secret dinner on the credit-card statement. I was shocked that you'd spent so much. I was also angry that you thought so much of her that you'd spoil her. I'm disappointed that you didn't think enough of me to treat me the same way.'

By contrast, emoting would start with waving the bill under your partner's nose: 'How could you? You bastard! Did you think of me? Our hard-earned money!' And that would probably just be the beginning of a hellish night together. When you report your feelings, you will calm down, the tension in the body will be released, you will be able to think more clearly, be properly heard and taken seriously. This approach could lead to an apology and probably a table at an even better restaurant.

Part two: Take it in turns to talk, listen and summarise

In this part of the exercise, the first partner has up to three minutes to make their case. The second partner must not interrupt or rehearse their side of the argument. They should just listen. When the first partner has finished (or their time is up), the second partner will summarise the main points of the argument. Don't answer these points, comment on them or analyse them, just report back what they have said. The first partner finishes their time in the talking spotlight by adding to the summary anything important that has been overlooked. Next, the two partners swap roles and the second partner talks while the first listens and then summarises. Once each party has fully understood the other's opinions and position, discuss your findings and how to move forward.

How to deal with panic attacks

Flashbacks to traumatic moments connected with your partner's affair can be overwhelming; here are four simple approaches to coping:

1. Acknowledge that you are panicking.
   - Self-talk yourself down.
   - 'I can cope with this' and 'I've been through this before'.

2. Focus on the situation and not on yourself.
   - Focus on concrete objects around you.
   - Describe them to yourself in detail.
   - How can you make yourself safer?
   - Hold on to something.
   - Sit down.

3. Take time-out.
   - Take a deep breath as this will relax your muscles and slow down your heart rate.
   - Have a good stretch.
   - Picture a relaxing scene where you feel safe. Use all your senses to make the place as real as possible.
   - Imagine someone that you trust talking to you. What advice are they giving?

4. Remind yourself that the attacks end.
   - They only last a few moments.
   - This feeling will not last.
   - You know this from experience.

Are you suffering from Post-traumatic Stress Disorder?

If you are still anxious, depressed or obsessive, there could be another problem. Here are the classic signs:

1. Irritability or outbursts of anger.
2. Difficulty concentrating.
3. Excessive vigilance – not only needing to know your partner's schedule but also checking their emails and text messages.
4. Difficulty falling or staying asleep.
5. Jumping at the slightest sound.
6. Physical reactions when reminded of the infidelity – like a story about cheating on a TV soap opera – and feelings of nausea or shakiness.

If you have two or more of these symptoms, and a month has passed since discovering your partner's infidelity, you should consult your doctor.

Question time

If you have become stuck in the polarised roles of Inquisitor and Accused, and your relationship has tipped back into crisis, this exercise will help you co-operate and start to like each other again.

1. The Inquisitor needs to accept that pushing for facts can be counterproductive and the Accused needs to accept that withdrawing, stonewalling or getting angry is not working either.

2. Set up a compromise contract where one short period a week becomes Question time – for example, an hour or two on a Wednesday night.
3. The Inquisitor cannot ask about the affair until Question time, or discuss the findings during the week.
4. In return, the Accused agrees to answer all questions – patiently, honestly and fully – which are asked during Question time but at no other time.
5. After a few weeks of questions and answers being contained in this manner, you will discover that you no longer need Question time. Celebrate by using the time where you would have discussed the affair for a shared treat.

Checkpoint

Three key points for surviving Stage Five: Attempted Normality

1. It takes months rather than weeks to fully recover from an affair.
2. Look at your own behaviour to see if there is anything that is stopping your partner from being open.
3. Write down your internal dialogue and check back for distortions, exaggerations and irrational leaps in logic.

Stage Six:
Despair – Bodies Float
to the Surface

RECOVERY

Despair – Bodies Float to the Surface

Attempted Normality

Hope

Decision Time

Intense Questioning

Shock and Disbelief

DISCOVERY

At the beginning of the book, I explained that an affair brings both danger and opportunity. At this stage in the recovery process, these two possibilities are finely balanced. The danger is all too clear. It is very easy for couples to become downcast. They worry that the affair has cast such a deep shadow that they can never return into the light. But what about the opportunity? It is hard to imagine anything positive coming out of an affair, so let me explain.

In every relationship there are unresolved issues, fundamental differences of opinion and shaky compromises. In most cases, couples muddle through by agreeing to differ, by closing their eyes, by downplaying the importance of something or burying the issues so deep that they are not really aware of them. I call these the 'dead bodies' in a relationship. Staying with this analogy, most couples know where the bodies are buried but decide not to disturb them. When I'm counselling couples who are not coping with infidelity, we often tiptoe round these sites and deal with the immediate problems at hand without needing to exhume the bodies. In effect, I look at what marital therapists call the 'presenting problems', help the couple communicate and understand each other better, and send two hopefully satisfied people off into the sunset.

However, it is different with infidelity couples. Their levels of distress are much higher, the desire never to experience this hell again greater, and a determination to 'get to the bottom of things' brings the dead bodies up to the surface. It is almost as if these issues have not been buried but weighted and thrown into a large lake. Everything on the surface might seem tranquil and beautiful but slowly, surely and unstoppably, these bodies float up to the top. As you can imagine, it is not a pretty sight. And when you

175

are dealing with the stresses of infidelity – doubly so. This is why I've called this stage 'Despair'. However, please take heart. This sixth stage is a necessary part of your journey and provides the *opportunity* to emerge with not only a healed relationship but also a happier, healthier and fundamentally better one.

Before I explain some of the bodies that have floated to the surface in other people's relationships, and provide some guidance as to what to expect in your own, I need to return to the equation about what causes affairs from chapter two.

Problem + Poor Communication + Temptation = Infidelity

While previously you might have put the 'problem' down to something immediately at hand (for example 'being too busy' or 'taking each other for granted'), at this stage you are beginning to look beyond the presenting problems to the fundamental drivers beneath them. These dead bodies tend to fall into three categories: known, discovered and hidden.

Dealing with 'known' bodies

In some relationships, the problems have been there from the start. In the first flush of love, these do not seem barriers at all – and overcoming them might even add to the passion – but once reality sinks in everything becomes more complex. A reasonably common example of a long-term 'known' problem would be step-parenting. Tracey and Paul, whom we met earlier, both had children from their previous marriages. Her son was older and left home shortly after they married. However, Paul's son was eleven and, although he lived with his mother, he spent alternate weekends with his father and Tracey. 'My son has never felt very welcome in our home – which puts me on edge – and I try extra hard to give him a good time. I used to hear this over-jolly tone in my voice and I'd hate that. It was not a good atmosphere,' Paul explained. 'Don't get me wrong. Tracey was never unpleasant, there was just this sense that my son was in the way. I sort of understood because she'd done her child-rearing and didn't want to start all over again.'

Over the years, Paul and Tracey had tried to discuss the problem but never found anything beyond an uneasy truce. 'Tracey would say: "This is who I am. Take it or leave it." And that's fine,' Paul explained, 'but deep down I was resentful and I suppose I used that resentment to justify my cheating.' Although I knew there were step-parenting issues from their initial first assessment interview, Paul and Tracey were not ready to face them until the last phase of their counselling. So I had to take the couple through the Shock, Intense Questioning, Decision-Making, Hope and Attempted Normality stages before they were ready to resolve the step-parenting.

Other relationships work reasonably well from the start but are derailed by circumstances; for example, one partner having to work away or the arrival of a second child. 'I felt terribly alone in my marriage,' explained Robert, 'she was tied up with the children and would give lip service to my bad day but the kids had to be bathed and put to bed. She wasn't as bad as my boss who kept on insisting "stop bringing me problems, bring me solutions" but it was like I always had to be strong to support Rosie. Who was there for me?'

In these child-centred relationships, the couple become Mummy and Daddy – rather than Husband and Wife – and all the emotional energy goes into family time and none into couple time. When Rosie looked back over the past few years, she could see why Robert had been attracted to a work colleague: 'It must have been nice to be wanted for himself, not as someone to fix the children's tea or ferry them somewhere. I would have liked that myself too.' Although they were both aware that the passion was slowly draining out of their marriage, they had done nothing about it. 'I thought it would get better as the children got older,' explained Rosie. 'I thought that's just the way it is,' said Robert. Fortunately, infidelity brought issues to a head and created a sense that something must be done.

Sometimes the 'known' problem is so overwhelming that it is not so much a buried body but a zombie that haunts the relationship. When George, fifty-three, had an affair with a younger work colleague, his wife, Vanessa, not only had to deal with the betrayal but also with the news that the other woman was expecting George's baby: 'Before the birth, I said I would try to include this child in my life and I meant it. But now that my husband has his new baby daughter – and you have no idea how much it hurts to say those words – I am finding it impossible to contemplate not only me being a part of her life but my husband being a part of her life, too. I suppose I have no right to stop him knowing his child if he wants.' At that point, George had only seen his daughter once. 'He thinks he should play some role in her life beyond financial provider; when I ask him what that means he can't really say, which doesn't help me either,' explained Vanessa.

Even when the problem is as fundamental as this one, it is important to go through the first stages of recovery. Vanessa and George needed to focus on improving their day-to-day communication and on discovering whether their original bond was strong enough to sustain them. So when they tried to discuss the reaction of their own children (in their twenties and away from home) to the news of their father's new daughter or some future event in the child's life, I banned the subject and kept them focused on their relationship and the immediate concerns of communicating about the next access visit. However, I could tell when they had reached Stage Six because of the despair in the counselling room: the bodies had began to float back up to the surface.

Occasionally, one partner has a secret buried body but the drama, the hours of talking, and the intense analysis following an affair, encourages a disclosure. Trudie and Jack, in their late thirties, had been married for almost twenty years and had two children together. Jack thought he knew everything about Trudie until, during the intense talking stage after his affair, she confessed to being sexually abused by an uncle: 'I can't remember how old I was, but I was probably about eight or nine. My mother did shift work and me and my sisters would go and sleep over at an aunt's house, and he'd come in and "check on me". It stopped when I was about thirteen and told him "hands off or I tell". Unpleasant at the time but I dealt with it.' Jack took the revelation more seriously: 'You've always held something back and never really let go when we make love. This all finally makes sense.'

Moving on

Many couples find the despair at this stage overwhelming, especially as most have tried everything to solve their long-term intractable disputes and nothing has changed. Sadly, some give up and declare their relationship broken beyond repair. This is a great pity because anyone who has truly engaged with the previous stages on the journey from discovery to recovery has learnt some important new skills: *Opening your mind* (problems are not black and white, right or wrong, and people are not good or bad, innocent or guilty); *Understanding* (you are more prepared to look at your share of the impasse rather than blame your partner); *Finding a positive out of a negative* (nothing is as bleak as you first imagine; there are pleasures, for example, from being a stepparent); *Looking beneath the surface* (instead of getting distracted by surface arguments, which often go round in pointless circles, you are ready to tackle real drivers of the problem); and *Confident and productive decision-making* (you have started to look at all the angles before finding a solution). The other benefit of tackling long-term 'known' problems after an affair is that each partner desperately wants to heal and therefore is more generous and flexible.

So if you are worried about the 'known' problems in your relationship, you could be in for a pleasant surprise. In many cases, when the dead bodies finally float to the surface, they have already lost their power to scare. Although my clients have spent weeks dreading this moment, it is frequently an anti-climax. Either the problem is solved in half a session or they have already found a solution at home.

This is what happened with Tracey and Paul's step-parenting dilemma. 'Paul's affair made me take a long, hard look at myself,' said Tracey. 'I have to admit that I was a bit of a bitch.' She made a conscious effort to get closer to Paul's son. This not only gave her a better relationship with her stepson but also made Paul reassess his behaviour, too. 'I realise that I was trying too hard when my son came over,' said Paul, 'I used to entertain him every single moment and couldn't just sit back from time-to-time and let him be.' There was another surprise side-effect. 'I've a much closer relationship with my own son,' said Tracey, 'I think I'm warmer and more tolerant of other people's failings – after all, I've discovered that I've quite a few of my own.'

What about more intractable issues where it is harder to find a middle way? The secret is just to *sit quietly with the problems* – nothing more. There is no attempt to persuade your partner or make them feel guilty. There is no attempt to resolve anything. Each partner just engages emotionally with the reality of the situation, with no distractions, no walking away and no sparing the other's feelings.

So what happened when Vanessa and George sat quietly with the issues over the 'affair baby'? 'It is extraordinary to watch how my daughter is beginning to form her own little personality. The tenacity when she pulls herself up on something and stands up. It's incredible,' said George. 'How can I walk away and desert her?' For the first time, Vanessa had to acknowledge that her husband had bonded with this baby: 'I guessed that something like this would happen but he's never really spoken about it before.' There was a short break in their counselling over Christmas. Afterwards, Vanessa asked for a one-to-one session. She had been feeling very down and wanted to sort out her feelings. I declined, explaining that her feelings should not be packaged up and hidden away but something that her husband needed to engage with too. During the next session, Vanessa sat quietly and expressed her feelings while George listened: 'I'm not so upset about the baby and that frightens me. I think I'm withdrawing. I don't think that I can cope. I will end up hurting everybody, my own children – who love us both dearly.' I asked her if she'd ever said this before. She replied, 'No, this is the first time.'

Instead of the previous intellectual debates, recriminations or arguments, they had simply expressed their feelings and acknowledged the depth of each other's emotions. They were finally ready to face the reality of their problems. (There will be more about this couple in the final chapter.)

Sitting quietly with the problem was also a breakthrough for Jack and Trudie and her childhood sexual abuse. Jack was very angry: 'I want to go round and punch his lights out. I want to make him suffer like Trudie has suffered. He's violated my whole family and he should be made to pay.' Trudie was upset too: 'This reaction is making it worse, much worse. I don't want to hurt my mum, she was doing the best that she could under difficult circumstances.' When they had truly acknowledged the depth of each other's feelings, they were able to reach a compromise. Jack agreed that there was no benefit in him going in 'ham-fisted', but Trudie agreed that she would stop 'trivialising' what happened and seek counselling.

So how can you and your partner truly acknowledge each other's feelings? A useful technique is 'sitting in your partner's shoes'. The idea is that you become a journalist and interview your partner about the issue at hand (with a genuine curiosity and an open mind). However, there is a twist: your partner pretends to be you and answers as he or she imagines that you would! So, using Robert and Rosie – the couple with a child-centred marriage – Robert became the neutral professional journalist and interviewed Rosie about having children but she replied as if she were him. He started with general questions (while they were both getting used to the idea) and then worked up to the specific issues. Here are some of his questions to her:

Hello, Robert, how did you feel when you first held your son?
How did having children affect you?
What changes did you notice in the way that your wife responded to you?
How were you feeling in the sixth months before the affair?
How did you feel towards your children during this time?

It is important that you do not come out of the character of 'professional journalist' and dispute what your partner says. Take a note of anything that she or he imagines to be true but is actually false. Remember to use the detached language of a journalist – it is 'your' children, not 'our' children. Try not to lead your partner but ask open questions – these are ones that start with 'How', 'Why', 'When', 'What'. Afterwards, clarify what your partner imagined incorrectly, discuss the overall experience of sitting in your shoes and what both of you have learnt. It takes a while to process this new knowledge, so don't change round immediately, but instead come back to the exercise the next day.

Dealing with 'discovered' bodies

An affair puts a mirror up to a relationship and many couples discover cracks of which they were completely unaware. I call these 'discovered' bodies and they can range from minor to potentially devastating issues. Starting at the easier end of the scale, couples often discover how isolated they have become. Paul – with the step-parenting issue – realised that he had no friends: 'I've never been very sociable. I prefer not to be friends with people at work – just keep them as colleagues. I didn't really like having people round to the house as I wanted it to be just Tracey and me. Looking back, that was not particularly healthy. It was unburdening myself to this woman at work that created the bond. Before I knew it, I was telling her secrets and she was telling me secrets. It was wrong.'

Other people discover that they had the wrong priorities in life. Certainly finding out about his wife's six-month affair made Carl, thirty-eight, stop short. He had a high-pressure job as a chef in a nationally known restaurant: 'I was entirely focused on getting on, getting good reviews and providing a good lifestyle for my family. I thought my wife was happy looking after the children – that was her focus.' He didn't realise how lonely she felt and that she'd rather be listened to than bought nice things. In the aftermath of her affair, Carl decided to make some changes. 'There was no need to put in quite so many hours. So I came home earlier, took my son to football practice, and began to discover all the things I'd neglected. Most importantly, my wife and I remembered that we really like spending time together.'

Behind many affairs, there is someone stuck in a rut; someone who finds life rather grey and predictable; someone who wants to feel truly alive again. So it is not surprising that the 'discovered' body for many couples is a mid-life crisis where the thrill of the chase, the adrenaline pump of deception and the easy passion of illicit sex had been covering an existential crisis: Who am I, what's the meaning of life and what shall I do with what's left of my life?

A study at the University of New Hampshire in the US found that forty-five is the most common age for women to have an affair and fifty-five for men. This corresponds with research at STI Clinics in the UK (Sexually Transmitted Infections) which found women aged between forty-five and fifty-four, and men between the age of fifty-five and sixty, had the highest rate of infection. In my research on 'Adultery in the UK', I found that the most common age of someone having an affair was forty-six. Taking stock around the mid-point in your life is always a good idea and most fulfilled people find that they need a fresh adventure. This could be training for a new job, taking up a demanding hobby, or travelling to exotic destinations. Unfortunately, some people think their partners will not be supportive, or they feel trapped by their expectations and become particularly vulnerable to an affair at this life stage.

Another by-product of infidelity is that it can bring up unexpected echoes from people's pasts and make them reassess aspects of their childhood. Anna is forty-one, and her husband left after his affair was discovered. However, despite ending the affair and returning home, he still kept texting the other woman and telling lies (for example, claiming that she had gone back to her husband when, in reality, they had split) and generally conducted a secret 'emotional' affair for the next six months. Relations between Anna and her husband were dark, destructive and very emotional. When they were exhausted and had nothing more to shout at each other, Anna started reading up about infidelity and reflecting on her past: 'When I was stressed – and ranted, lost control, said hurtful things or tried to control him – I would apologise over and over again and I'd say, "I'll do whatever you want." Suddenly, I had a flashback to my mother doing this when she tried to stop my father from hitting her.'

Margaret, from the second chapter, who threw her husband out of the house at knife point, discovered problems in her relationship with her parents: 'When I finally told my mother what happened, her first reply was, "I'm glad that you didn't cry when you told me because I don't think I could have dealt with that" and her only comment since has been when she saw me not wearing my wedding ring: "When is this silliness going to stop?". When I told my father he replied that it was something most men did and my tragedy was that I found out.' Margaret had always known that her relationship with her parents had been superficial but their lack of support meant that she could no longer ignore it.

Returning to Paul again, he had to reassess his relationship with his mother after returning home for a family birthday: 'My mother took Tracey aside and told her how she had nearly walked out on my father over his affairs. He actually told her to leave but that he wouldn't let her take the children and we were only little,' Paul explained. 'I'd always taken my father's side, because he was the life and soul of the party, while my mother had seemed rather miserable. Now, I truly understand why.' The aftermath of an affair makes both partners question everything and approach not just their relationship, but their whole lives, with fresh eyes.

Moving on

The good news, if you are dealing with a 'discovered body', is that these problems are reasonably straightforward to solve. Once all the issues are out in the daylight, it is often obvious how to move forward. Paul decided to invite some work colleagues round to the house and to get to know them better. He also joined a local photography club to meet new people. Finally, he apologised to his mother for not being more understanding in the past.

Once Anna understood why she kept on at the same failed strategy, she found it easier to break free: 'I used to keep on pushing for things, I have learnt to step back and wait.' Margaret found it harder to forge a new relationship with her parents – they were elderly and stuck in their ways. However, she was more honest about her feelings and this allowed all three of them to get along better. If you want to achieve something similar, follow this three-step process:

1. *Keep your comments focused on today.* For example: 'I found what you said hurtful because . . .' Don't get sidetracked into listing old failings – even if they are examples of the same issue. Your parents cannot change the past and it is easy for them to be overwhelmed with guilt and become defensive.
2. *Follow up with reassurance.* The idea is to both explain why you're having this conversation and to offer an olive branch. For example: 'I'm sure you did it for all the best reasons', or 'I'm saying this because I love you and want us to be closer.'
3. *Make a deal for a better future.* This should be practical and easy to monitor. For example, 'Let's talk on the telephone more often', or 'If I do something that irritates you, please say as I'd rather have it out in the open', or 'I'll try to be less sensitive but I'd be grateful if you didn't bring up . . .' Deals where both parties get something that they want are more likely to stick.

Dealing with 'hidden' bodies

Some problems are buried so deeply that neither partner is aware what caused the infidelity. This is not only perplexing but also frightening. However, in my experience, the hidden body is normally one of three problems – which don't just affect couples dealing with infidelity. Fortunately, they are reasonably straightforward to solve:

Inequality

Good relationships are made up of two equal partners. Sometimes, one partner will have more power in one particular area but it is balanced by the other having more power somewhere else. An example would be the traditional marriage where a man went out to work and looked after money and practical things while the woman stayed at home and looked after the family and emotional matters. However, when power gets polarised in this way, it can often lead to great unhappiness – especially when couples reach their middle years. For example, Carl (the chef from earlier) felt resentful that his wife excluded him from decisions about the children and belittled his suggestions of how to spend family time together. Conversely, when his wife, Sandy, decided to train as an aerobics instructor, she felt that he didn't take her work seriously and that he could never be counted on to look after their youngest child. Therefore, she felt unsupported and resentful.

How does inequality feed into infidelity? I find that a lot of people who have affairs – and especially women – are exhausted givers. They feel that they put a lot into their relationship and get very little back. This is certainly how Sandy saw things in her marriage: 'I know it is selfish but I saw my affair as something for me. A little reward after spending so much time and energy running after someone else; it was so wonderful to be noticed.' Interestingly, the person who is not putting enough energy into a relationship can also be vulnerable to an affair. They are already less committed and have one foot out of the relationship.

A big power imbalance is often another cause of infidelity. The more powerful partner will expect to have all his or her needs met – like sex, when away on business. This sense of entitlement is one of the reasons why celebrities are so prone to infidelity. The less powerful partner – or the person who perceives themselves as less powerful – will feel resentful and become prone to temptation too.

Phoebe and Adam met through work, they were both in their twenties and earning similar amounts of money. Their relationship worked very well. However, five years later, Phoebe became pregnant and gave up work: 'I had a difficult birth, suffered from post-natal depression, and my confidence went through the floor. While Adam would go off to work in a nicely pressed suit, I'd have a day covered in baby sick. Previously, I'd had my own money and never had to justify anything. Although his money was our money, I felt guilty spending anything on me.' She ended up having an affair with a friend's husband. 'I felt guilty, excited and angry with myself but more sexually charged than I had been in a long time. I could look into my lover's eyes and see the desire and how he'd risk everything for me.' In effect, she felt powerful again.

There will be more about balancing unequal relations in the next chapter, but I find the best way to help unequal couples is to focus on the way they talk to each other and this is the topic of my next hidden body.

Talking at cross purposes

Transactional Analysis, or TA for short, was founded in the fifties by an American psychiatrist called Eric Berne. He proposed that all our thoughts, feelings and behaviour come from three distinct parts of our personality: 'Parent', 'Adult' and 'Child'. (The idea is similar to Freud's super ego, ego and id.) The most important thing to stress is that all three parts are equally important and are needed at different times. The 'Parent' part comes in two types: Nurturing (caring and kind) and Critical (strict and firm). The 'Child' also comes in two types: Free (creative and fun) and Adapted (anxious to please, sulky or rebellious). In contrast, there is one sort of 'Adult' which is rational, thoughtful and considerate. When you and your partner are both using the same part of your personality, everything works smoothly. For example, you've both been invited to a slightly stuffy party and your inner Child meets the eye of your partner's inner Child and both decide to put some music on and get everybody dancing. Berne calls this a *Concordant Transaction*. A variation on this relatively straight-forward type of communication is when one partner's inner child complains: 'I'll never get all these done', and the other's Nurturing

Parent will reply: 'Never mind, I'll sort it out.' This is called a *Parallel Transaction* and, in theory, this kind of communication could continue happily for years.

The problems come from what Berne calls *Crossed Transactions*. For example, the Adult part of your personality asks: 'Have you seen my keys?' However, instead of replying with his or her inner Adult, your partner responds: 'You shouldn't leave things lying about' – which is the critical part of Parent – or 'Why do you blame me for everything?' which is the adapted part of Child. Incidentally, it is not just the words that betray which part of our personality is to the fore but the tone of voice, facial expressions and general body language.

The key to using TA, and avoiding *Crossed Transactions*, is spotting which part of your personality is in play. The following table should help:

	Parent		Adult	Child	
	Critical Parent	*Nurturing Parent*		*Free Child*	*Adapted Child*
Words	Should, don't, you can't, if I were you	Let me help you, don't worry, there-there	How, when, why, what are the facts, options	Wow, brilliant, you'll never guess	Sorry, if only, it's not my fault
Tones of voice	Stern, harsh, judgemental, indignant	Soothing, soft, caring, sympathetic	Clear, enquiring, assertive	Laughter, energetic, excited	Appealing, placating, protesting
Body language	Finger-pointing, hands on hips, rolling eyes upwards	Open arms, nodding, touching	Level eye contact, confident appearance, active listening	Bright-eyed, exaggerated motions, spontaneous	Downcast eyes, pouting, slumped shoulders

When someone decides to give into temptation and has an affair, they are often in Adapted Child mode. (This is why unfaithful partners come across like sulky, demanding and selfish teenagers.) If they were in the Adult part of their personality, they would say: 'I'm unhappy; we need to do something about our relationship.' So what stops them? Unfortunately, they probably expect to be greeted by their partner in Critical Parent mode: 'I do everything for you and you're still not happy' or 'You can't expect life to be all wine and roses.' In fact, the most common *Crossed Transaction* is Critical Parent/Adapted Child and, returning to the previous hidden body, it is also a sign that a couple has an unequal relationship. So what can be done?

- Learn to recognise which mode you and your partner are using. It helps to name them. 'That sounded so Critical Parent' or 'Am I playing Adapted Child?'
- If you don't like your partner's response, check which part of your personality you've used. If you sometimes think that you've got an extra child in the house, it could be that you are talking to your partner as Critical Parent. If your partner speaks to you as if you were six years old, it could be because you're responding as Adapted Child. In both cases, it would be better to switch into the Adult mode.
- Your partner's response is likely to match the mode that you employ. So if you use Adult, your partner will reply back as an Adult. If you use Free Child – let's be wicked and sneak off to bed in the middle of the afternoon – they will probably respond in a similar manner.

This technique is particularly useful for couples where one party – or sometimes both – feel there is a power imbalance. If you talk to and treat your partner as an equal, he or she will feel like one and begin to behave like one.

Your children's life stages

The third hidden body explains times when you feel restless, upset or anxious but can never quite put your finger on the reasons why. In fact, the feelings are so subtle that it is hard to pin them down at all. The whole experience is so difficult to categorise and normal problem-solving techniques are so hopeless that many people ignore the warning signs. Yet something is happening deep inside your gut and however busy you keep, the feelings keep gnawing away. Sometimes I think people in this situation launch into an affair because at least they understand the simple, bold feelings of desire, shame and guilt. So what's going on?

Perhaps the best way to explain this hidden body is to use an example. Adrian, thirty-eight, sought help because he was having a reckless affair with a former work colleague: 'I feel such a fool and such a bastard. My wife is expecting a baby and really needs me but I kept slipping out to meet this woman.' 'How do you feel about becoming a father,' I asked? 'We've already got two kids and really, that's enough,' he replied. He had told his wife about his misgivings but she was unsympathetic and told him to get used to the idea. 'I really feel that we're making a big mistake,' he sighed and buried his head in his hands.

When we looked at his family tree, I discovered that he was the third child in his family and that his parents had split up when he was about six. 'Why did your parents get divorced?' I asked. He just shrugged and I immediately had a picture of a confused little boy. 'Did you think it was something to do with you?' I asked. 'Not entirely, there were long-term problems and they were always arguing,' he replied, 'but I think I put an extra strain on them.' I articulated the feelings that were etched on his face: 'Maybe if you hadn't been born?' Slowly, Adrian nodded. Obviously, he wasn't responsible for his parents divorce but he had been carrying all these feelings buried deep inside. The impending birth of his own third child had brought this hidden body back up to the surface.

In the case of many couples, where I can't find what has brought something to a head, I look at their family trees and ask about what happened when they were the age that their children are now. Time and again, I find some important echo from the past.

Our sons and our daughters carry so many of our hopes and fears, that their struggles can impact on us even if we sailed through their particular life stage ourselves without too many problems. So what common life events can prompt infidelity?

- A child going off to school, and tasting independence for the first time, can make us long to be more independent.
- A moody teenager coping with their first crush or broken heart is difficult enough, even when your own marriage is strong. However, if you are even vaguely disappointed, it is easy to become nostalgic for your own teens or envious of your children's energy, looks or belief in their own immortality. This life stage is all about testing boundaries and discovering what is right or wrong. It is a time of rebellion and throwing caution to the wind – and the mood is infectious. This is why many parents, when their children are teenagers, step over the boundaries themselves and commit adultery.
- When children become young adults and vacate the nest, a relationship centred around being parents can feel directionless and empty. The temptation to flee – even if only temporarily into the third party's arms – can be overwhelming.

The best way of dealing with echoes from your children's life stage is to voice them out loud. This is hard because nobody likes to admit that they are jealous or identify with their children quite so closely. However, it can be an important breakthrough. Adrian began to make sense of his feelings of doom. He stopped the affair and used his own experiences of being the third child as a way of reintroducing the topic with his wife. Finally, he was able to admit that, however much he identified with this particular child, he and the baby were separate people and that history did not have to repeat itself. Time and again, admitting to a feeling or talking about a hidden body in the cold light of day – rather than letting things lurk in the shadows – will turn a difficult problem into harmless dust.

Even if your partner is not ready to acknowledge the echoes from the past, just getting him or her to tell stories from that particular era can be liberating. Ask for plenty of detail and the reactions of her or his parents, and afterwards discuss any similarities to today. In many cases, these discussions will be enough to cast fresh light on to the hidden body and to exorcise it. Other people find new, practical solutions for dealing with their children and reduce the overall tension in the house and, in that way, rebury the body for the time being.

Dealing with low self-esteem

One of the issues that comes to the surface during the Despair stage is self-esteem. It goes without saying that your partner's affair will do nothing for your confidence or feelings of self-worth. However, the issues around self-esteem are often more complex than at first sight. Once again, a case history is the best way to explain what's happening.

Danielle, forty-three, had put on a considerable amount of weight during her marriage. Since discovering her husband's infidelity, Danielle had lost two stone: 'He says he fancies me and will do so even more when I'm thinner, but still criticises my weight regularly, and often in public, to everyone's embarrassment. He even did it during an interview for a job in Scotland – where they had invited wives to come along and see the set-up. I was talking to his would-be boss about how I was excited to move up there as I would like to ski again. He interrupted to say I would have to lose a ton of weight before I could do that! I know he really detests overweight women, and often compares me with his stepmum whom he hated and who was overweight. He treated her like she was weak and stupid. I feel that I am tarred with the same brush.'

It is easy to see why Danielle was depressed and suffering from low self-esteem. However, her husband, Liam, had self-esteem problems too. The attention of the other woman had been flattering and temporarily made him feel better about himself. However, when Danielle discovered the affair, and the full reality of what he had done hit him, Liam's opinion of himself plummeted even lower. Unfortunately, instead of facing up to these difficult feelings, he unwittingly dumped all his unhappiness on to Danielle; and, by making her so utterly miserable by comparison, he felt a little bit better himself. After all, in his head, it was not his fault because it was her weight!

This tendency to treat someone else as a blank screen to play out our own needs and emotions is called 'projection'. Instead of trying to have a better relationship with his stepmother, or sorting out his childhood issues, Liam had projected his problems on to Danielle and attacked her. So what can be done? First, I helped Danielle understand that she was not responsible for Liam's poor relationship with his stepmum. However much weight she lost, the original problem would remain unaddressed. So I got her to say out loud and repeat: 'I am not Liam's stepmum.'

Next, she needed to understand why she was such an easy target for Liam to project on to. 'It's because I don't like carrying this much weight. I'm very sensitive even if someone looks at me a bit strangely. I think they're thinking "fat cow",' she explained. It was almost as if Danielle had hooks ready for Liam to hang his baggage on to. So I asked her how someone who felt comfortable about their weight might respond to Liam's comments: 'You're not exactly body beautiful yourself,' she laughed. In effect, she had begun to dismantle her hooks and the next time Liam tried to hang some of his old issues on her, they dropped harmlessly on to the floor.

Finally, she encouraged Liam to start afresh with his stepmother and have an Adult-to-Adult relationship.

If projection sounds familiar, follow this simple plan:

1. Recognise when someone is dumping their unhappiness or issues on to you.
2. Accept that these do not belong to you. However much you love someone, it is not your responsibility to solve all their problems.
3. Mentally remove the hooks. When someone says something potentially stinging, tell yourself: 'This is nothing to do with me.'
4. Encourage your partner to look at themselves. In a quiet moment take the hurtful comment and ask how he or she feels about that particular issue.

When it comes to dealing with your own self-esteem issues, ask yourself the following questions:

Are my current goals realistic? Write down all the things that you are currently beating yourself up for not achieving and check if you expect too much of yourself. For example, do you feel that you should be further along the recovery journey – even though it is only weeks or a couple of months since the affair was revealed? Most couples take about six months to reach this point.

Are you angry with yourself? After adultery, many Discoverers berate themselves for not spotting the signs earlier, for not being 'good enough' or for personal failings that contributed to their partner's infidelity. Is your criticism really justified? Would you have had to have second sight or an unnaturally suspicious mind? Have you been taking on more than your fair share of blame for what happened? Perhaps there is still a residue of anger that needs to be expressed towards your partner. (If this sounds risky, look back at the exercise 'Getting on the same page' in the previous chapter and in particular the idea of reporting feelings rather than just emoting.)

Have you down played your achievements in getting so far down the road? When you are tired, it is easy to overlook just how strong, capable or resilient you have been. Sadly, many people with low self-esteem discount or forget their achievements in reaching Stage Six and concentrate on what still needs to be done. If this sounds familiar, write a list of what you have learnt, how you have surprised yourself and the strengths you have discovered in yourself over the past few months.

Are you frightened about tackling some difficult issue between yourself and your partner? If anger is one of the most important underlying feelings that feeds low self-esteem, another is fear. So look at the buried bodies in your relationship and consider finally facing them. Remember, putting off something difficult not only lowers self-esteem but also leaves you feeling trapped.

Facing down your fears

It is natural to be frightened by infidelity. It brings up all sorts of difficult feelings: rejection, loss, vulnerability, pain, losing face and failure. As the bodies start to float to the surface, people fear that there is more to come, and still more. However, time and again, when my clients face up to the truth, the confrontation is never as bad as they expected. This is because our fear is often at its greatest just before the body reaches the surface. 'My heart was beating like hailstones on a tin roof,' said Danielle after she faced Liam about his put-downs about her weight. 'However, I discovered there were all sorts of things he didn't like about the way he looked too. He'd been small and not good at games at school and the other boys would pick on him.' As Liam remembered, and started to cry, Danielle felt a surge of joy: 'Something was finally being done. We were no longer poking each other with sharp sticks but starting to talk.' Often the greater the fear before talking, the greater the relief afterwards.

If you are still fearful, break the challenge into smaller steps by answering the following questions:

- What am I actually frightened of?
- How might I be exaggerating or distorting the challenge?
- What will I lose by not tackling my fear?
- What resources can I draw on to help me?
- What's the worst thing that could happen?
- How could I cope with that?
- How will I feel after I have faced my fear?

If you are fearful because your attempts to solve long-running problems have reared up and bitten you – or because it is impossible to accept the depth of your partner's feelings – this is probably a sign that maybe you have more to learn. If this is the case, you have two options. You could go back and try the exercises in the previous chapter or you could focus on some of the good things about your relationship.

Give your relationship a lift

This has been a particularly difficult stage, so it is important to balance the negative with the positive. To prevent your relationship becoming overwhelmed with despair, try these three revitalising strategies:

Recall the past. Instead of forever talking about problems or going over the affair, remember a good time from the past. The day that you first met is a good idea. Go over the story in detail, bring it to life with all the treasured details and relive the happiness again.

Use shared jokes. Every relationship has those little sayings that mean everything to the couple and nothing to anyone else. So use lines from your favourite movies and corny one-liners (for example, 'I only married you for your money') to remember your shared heritage.

Plan a treat. This should not be too elaborate or too far into the future (that comes later). Examples would be a meal in a favourite restaurant, a day out at a beauty spot or a concert. These treats will show that you can still have fun together and your whole relationship has not been swallowed up by intense conversations.

For the Discovered:
Despair – Bodies Float to the Surface

- The first steps on the journey from discovery to recovery are different for the Discoverer and the Discovered. However, by this stage, both partners feel the same despair. From now onwards, it is worth reading – if you have not started already – the main sections as well as these boxes.

- In some ways, an affair is a signal that something is wrong in a relationship. At this stage, those problems finally start to float to the surface. Although this process is painful, there are important lessons to be learnt.

- Think about what you liked about yourself in the affair. How were you different? If a new relationship allowed you to experiment and discover new things about yourself, how could you bring this new knowledge out of affair-bubble-world and into the real world?

- If you are looking to make fundamental changes to your life – perhaps after discovering a mid-life crisis – it is important to discuss options with your partner and give him or her an opportunity to express concerns or fears. Reaching a conclusion together, rather than presenting a fait accompli – will provide a much needed boost for your relationship.

- If your partner seems surly, it is often a sign of muffled sorrow or pain. Look beyond your partner's immediate mood, show compassion and reassure them that you do care. You will reap the benefit.

- Cutting off all meaningful contact with the third party will have allowed your relationship to grow stronger. However, at this point, the full loss of your affair partner will hit home. It might be tempting to send a casual email but this will reopen wounds and risk derailing your still-fragile relationship with your partner. But do not panic. Thinking about the third party and facing up to the loss is normal and often the beginning of the healing process. (For more information see 'Mourning the loss' in the exercise section.)

- This is a tough stage but it is truly the darkest hour before the dawn.

New skill: Acceptance

For most couples the bodies that appear during Stage Six are familiar or ultimately no great surprise. Many have repeatedly tried to find a resolution but one or both partners were angry, hurt, unreceptive or dismissive: 'She didn't really mean it', or 'If he thinks I'll do that, he's going to have to think again.' However, in the aftermath of infidelity, people are often prepared to listen and engage with the problems. As the American psychologist and philosopher William James (1842–1910) wrote: 'Acceptance of what has happened is the first step to overcoming the consequences of any misfortune.' Time and again, I find that once someone feels truly heard and their pain or hopes, in all their complexity, are acknowledged then a breakthrough is just a heartbeat away.

So how do you reach this point? The answer is simpler than most people imagine: stillness. We worry that, once our partner has laid out his or her problems, we will have to solve them. (This is what makes us so anxious or tempted to walk away.) In reality, there's no need to say anything. Words are completely secondary and, if required, will come out of the stillness. You just have to *accept* that this is what your partner feels and, from her or his viewpoint, these feelings are perfectly valid. That is all. No more. Just sit there, unblinking, and accept. It sounds easy but in our world of a million distractions – places to be and money to earn – fully engaged and freely given time is the greatest gift. And this is the miracle – when you give up trying to change someone, they stop having to defend themselves and finally become open to changing.

Summary

- By Stage Six, couples are ready to look beyond the obvious to the fundamental problems and unhappiness that causes affairs.
- If you feel overwhelmed, look back at the skills that you have already accumulated.
- Problems fit into three categories: known bodies (long-term and seemingly insoluble problems), discovered bodies (issues thrown up by the infidelity), and hidden bodies (these are often buried in the unconscious of each partner and need to be brought up to the surface).
- This stage can put the focus not only on your childhood but also on how you relate to your children. It is important to work closely with your partner as a team of two Adults, rather than as one Parent and a rebellious Child. Discuss contentious issues together in private, so that you provide a united front to your son or daughter.
- Often, the only thing you have to fear is fear itself.
- When a difficult or contentious body floats to the surface, look it fully in the face. From out of the stillness, a compromise will emerge.

Exercises

Say the unsayable . . . and be heard

In many relationships, there is a central problem that has not properly been addressed. Often both partners are aware of its existence, but it has only come up in anger (and therefore been ignored) at the height of an argument (so not properly heard) or leaked out in lots of small ways over minor issues (which were seen in isolation and therefore the severity of the problem has not registered).

So what is the alternative? Here are seven steps:

- *Be brave.* In many cases, when one partner calmly lays out their unsayable problem – and expresses a desire to work on it – the other partner may be upset but generally relieved to have everything out in the open.
- *Think it through.* Make certain that you are telling your partner something or some behaviour that he or she can work on or change (for example, to be more independent). By contrast, 'I never really fancied you' or 'I only got married because my parents wanted it' is cruel and pointless. If you are in any doubt, discuss it with a close friend first.
- *Name the feeling.* Being angry, bitter or disappointed with your partner is okay. It is impossible for two people to live together without experiencing these feelings at some point. Rather than letting the problem sneak out in sly put-downs or explode out as insults and aggressive behaviour, try telling your partner. For example: 'I feel angry' or 'I feel insecure' (remember to own the feeling and not to blame your partner).
- *Limit the feeling.* Unless you explain 'when', there is a danger your partner might misinterpret or draw the wrong conclusions. For example: '. . . when you don't listen' or '. . . when you would rather be somewhere else'.

- *Explain the feeling.* This is about spelling out why you feel this way. For example: '. . . because I think you don't care' or '. . . because I have been rejected before'.
- *Put it all together.* Now you have a three-part formula for effective communication: 'I feel..........when you.......... because..........' For example: 'I feel alone when you refuse to go on exotic or unusual holiday destinations because that's when I feel most alive.'
- *Reassure.* After telling your partner something difficult, it is important to offer some reassurance and check out his or her feelings. For example, 'I only said something because I think we have to be honest if we're going to save this relationship' or 'How do you feel about that?'

Refresh your belief structure

Our life is underpinned by hundreds of different beliefs acquired from our parents, our schools, our friends, the culture around us and our experiences. It is useful to bring these beliefs up from our subconscious into the light of day and examine them to see if any of them are out of date. It is particularly important for someone with low self-esteem because an unduly negative belief structure can really hold us back. What do I mean by a belief? These are sayings that we accept as the truth. For example, 'You can't teach an old dog new tricks', 'There's no such thing as a free lunch', 'Life's not fair', 'There is always someone worse off than yourself' or 'It's always my fault'.

1. Take a piece of paper and write down as many beliefs as possible. Start with those from your childhood. I'll start you off in each category with some of my own: 'I want doesn't get' and 'Family hold back'. Next add those from school: 'You're average' (we were streamed according to ability and I was always in the middle). If you went to college, university or had job training, what new beliefs did you acquire? 'Life is a sh*t sandwich, the more bread you have the less sh*t you have to eat' (this was written on the toilet

walls at my university in the seventies). What about your
friends: 'What doesn't kill us makes us stronger.' From the
wider culture: 'If you're not careful you'll be living in a
bus shelter and eating your own shoe leather'; and, finally,
add beliefs garnered from your own life experiences: 'I can
always cope if I take things one week at a time' (bereavement
after my first partner died).

2. Once you have about twenty or thirty plus examples,
   go through your beliefs and count up the number that
   are enabling (positive) and how many are disabling
   (negative). This is particularly important if you have low
   self-esteem, as most sufferers have significantly more
   disabling beliefs.

3. Question the validity of these beliefs. For example, the one
   on the toilet wall at university: are the rich really happier?
   Don't we need some difficult or unpleasant experiences
   to grow?

4. Which beliefs are distorted or out of date? For example,
   when I worked as a life guard in a holiday camp during
   the summer break from university, I met lots of people
   who left school with few or no qualifications. I had been
   comparing myself only to my immediate peers. In effect, I
   was not average.

5. How could you recast some of these beliefs? Perhaps 'I
   want doesn't get' could become 'If you don't ask, nobody
   knows what you need.'

6. Where could you get some new, positive beliefs? For
   example, from this book: 'Good things can come out of
   bad experiences', and from my other books, 'You can
   fall back in love' (*I Love You, But I'm Not in Love with
   You*, published by Bloomsbury), and 'There's someone
   for everybody' (*The Single Trap: The Two-Step Guide
   to Escaping It and Finding Lasting Love*, published by
   Bloomsbury). Nearly every film has a message – mainly
   uplifting – so think about your favourites and which beliefs
   you could adopt from them.

Mourning the loss

Although the physical side of the affair will be over and contact cut (or reduced to business matters only if the affair was with a work colleague), many discovered partners find that they still 'have feelings' for the third party. This exercise has been designed to help extinguish those final remnants. However, it will also work for a Discoverer who needs to mourn the loss of their pre-affair relationship – which had seemed so safe and secure – and clear the decks for a new and better relationship with their partner.

1. *Put away things with strong memories.* If you've had the affair, you have hopefully thrown away all presents, letters and other love tokens. However, it is often necessary to go further. (For example, stop driving past places with strong memories – like the bar where you would rendezvous with your lover.) If you are the Discoverer, you might want to put away things that feel tainted by your partner's deception. (For example, a snap shot from what might have seemed like a happy holiday together but then subsequently you learnt that your partner had already started his or her affair.)

2. *Don't wallow.* For the Discovered, this means switching channels when the third party's favourite singer comes on the radio. For the Discoverer, change channels when the talk show is about cheating. There is no point in torturing yourself.

3. *Use distraction techniques.* Instead of allowing a daydream of how things might have been to take hold, think about something practical and pressing: what to cook for supper or when the car is due for a service.

4. *Re-integrate the experience back into your life.* When someone is special in our lives, we will often give them a particular role. For example, a grandmother might be the only person for whom you can do no wrong or your father might be the protective force that allows no harm to come your way. After a bereavement, the final part of

the healing comes when we can take back that role and, for example, look after or value ourselves. If you were unfaithful, think about what your affair partner meant. Perhaps he helped with your career? In that case, how could you progress your career yourself? (Maybe talk to human resources about a training course.) Perhaps she made you feel young again? In that case, why not follow those old teenage ambitions that were cast aside. (Maybe you could buy a guitar and take lessons.) If you were the Discoverer, think about what your pre-affair relationship symbolised. Perhaps your partner 'rescued' you from a difficult place. How could you start to take more responsibility yourself?

Checkpoint

Three key points for surviving Stage Six:
Despair – Bodies Float to the Surface

1. This is an opportunity to change your relationship for the better.
2. Really listen to your partner and walk in his or her shoes. What if every word she or he said was true?
3. Think about one small positive change. What would be the first step towards making it happen?

Stage Seven:
Intense Learning

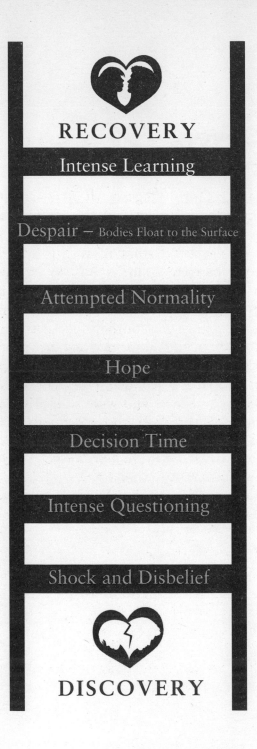

RECOVERY

Intense Learning

Despair – Bodies Float to the Surface

Attempted Normality

Hope

Decision Time

Intense Questioning

Shock and Disbelief

DISCOVERY

As couples reach the final stage of the recovery process, their love has begun to be renewed and they feel closer than they have for a long time. There is a lot to celebrate but many people feel uncertain or worried: 'What if we slip back?', 'How can I be sure it won't happen again?' or 'I can see myself starting to trust again but it's still hard.' If this sounds familiar, rest assured. It is common to have doubts or a small crisis of confidence towards the end of the journey. The best way to address these fears is to look at the major reasons that people stray and inoculate your relationship against them. Turkish psychologists Zuhal Yenicen and Dogan Kökdemir asked over four hundred students (a mixture of those who were single, in a relationship, and a few who were married) about infidelity. Thirty-six per cent had direct experience of infidelity either as the 'betrayer' or the 'betrayed' and overall, the students gave a hundred different reasons for being unfaithful (*Social Behaviour and Personality*, 2006). The answers were grouped into six categories and ranked from most to least common:

Legitimacy
- Partner does not show any involvement in the relationship
- Seeing no future in the relationship
- Partner is insensitive
- Relationship is a mistake
- For revenge
- This justification was more likely to be used by women

Seduction
- The 'betrayer' was led on by someone beautiful or handsome
- Overwhelming desire for another person
- This justification was more likely to be used by men

Normalisation
- It's fashionable
- Everybody's doing it
- A natural human right
- Men thought this a reason for women to commit adultery

Sexuality
- Having a poor sexual relationship
- Partner unwilling to have sexual relations
- Partner made unjustified sexual demands (for example, a taboo activity)
- Interestingly, men used this justification and projected their feelings on to women and wrongly imagined that this factor was important for them too

Social background
- Married too young
- Growing up in a conservative social culture
- Having too few romantic relationships during adolescence

Sensation
- Seeking enjoyment
- Boredom with routine life

In my opinion, the top two reasons, legitimacy and seduction, are the most important. In effect, normalisation and social background would not come into play unless the straying partner did not feel that he or she had legitimate reasons. Likewise, someone is only vulnerable to being seduced if there are sexuality or sensation issues in their relationship. So how can you use this knowledge to protect your relationship? Later in the chapter, I will explain how to deal with seduction (the three fundamentals of a good sex life), but first it is important to build a strong foundation and improve communication to counteract legitimacy.

The four fundamentals of a good relationship

As Leo Tolstoy famously wrote at the beginning of his novel *Anna Karenina*: 'Happy families are all alike; every unhappy family is unhappy in its own way.' But what qualities do these happy families share which allow them to work through their problems rather than be sunk by them? Unfortunately, happy families provide little drama and therefore seldom appear in books or movies. Fortunately, I have had the privilege of helping hundreds of couples shift from being unhappy to happy. I know my task is complete when they begin to acquire and value these four key skills:

Listening and talking

The first skills will come as no surprise. When many couples arrive in my therapy office, one partner will complain: 'He never talks to me' or 'She shuts me out'. Talking about problems is important, but this truth has become so self-evident that many people overlook the equally vital skill of listening. Time and again, the person complaining that their partner is uncommunicative, and never tells them anything, will interrupt when he or she begins to open up! (In the talker's mind, there is just one more important fact or example that needs to be communicated before she or he can listen.) Meanwhile, the quieter partner feels persecuted and becomes more and more silent. However, the better a talker becomes at listening, in turn, the better the other partner will become at communicating. Here are a few tips:

- A good listener is prepared to hear things that are uncomfortable or unpleasant.
- A good listener will ask for more information and check they have heard correctly and not jump to conclusions.
- A good listener will not use the time their partner is speaking to rehearse their side of the argument.
- A good listener will first accept that their partner's viewpoint is valid (from where he or she is standing) and then give his or her contrary opinion.

Once the matching skills of listening and talking are in place, it is extraordinary how much each partner will open up and how much can be achieved.

Paul and Tracey, whom we met in chapters two, four and six, discovered a lot when they talked and listened to each other about their previous sexual partners. 'The subject had been off-limits before,' said Tracey, 'not so much out of jealousy but because of our own insecurity.' So what had they discovered? 'I'd only had sex on two occasions when I didn't think or hope that this would be a long-term relationship and afterwards I felt dirty and degraded,' she explained.

'I'd been brought up a good Catholic and the reverend brothers had made sure that we didn't stray,' said Paul. 'So when I got to the freedom of university, I went wild and put it around quite a lot.'

Listening to Paul, Tracey began to understand that although she could not separate love and sex, for Paul it was something different: 'It was just a physical act.' This provided her with a fresh perspective on his infidelity. 'It's not like he bought her presents or took her off somewhere special – that's the sort of thing that would really have upset me.'

Accepting that your partner has a different take on some-thing important – and learning to live with that difference – is a very adult take on life and it provided Paul and Tracey with an important building block in their recovery. The final piece of learning was more for Paul than for Tracey. 'I remember the atmosphere in the house when my mother didn't "put out" – she was terrified of getting pregnant again – and how resentful my Dad would get. I'd also notice – over Christmas and Easter when we were around more – how the mood would lighten if she relented.' As an adult, Paul had also sulked if Tracey was too tired or not interested. 'It made me realise that I'd acted as if I was entitled, which is not really the right approach for fulfilling lovemaking.'

Bringing up problems and containing

How well a couple settle disputes – rather than their compatibility, similar values or a healthy sex life – is the best indicator of which relationships will thrive and which will fail. Psychologist John Gottman, from the University of Washington in Seattle, set up a marital lab – a comfortably furnished apartment with kitchen, living room and bedroom – not only to watch couples interact but also to monitor their heart rates, pulse and how much they sweat under stress. After studying two thousand married couples over twenty years, he claims a 94 per cent accuracy in predicting who will stay married. Gottman not only refutes the idea that frequent arguments lead to divorce but also goes one step further: 'Occasional discontent, especially during a marriage's early years, seems to be good for the union in the long run.'

In every relationship, one partner tends to bring up issues; yet the other's role is equally important but often misunderstood. Liza and Bob are in their late twenties, and like many couples complained about 'communication problems' – normally a code for 'our arguments solve nothing'. In their first counselling session, Bob looked virtuous: 'If something needs to be said, I will be the one to do it.' He then cast Liza in the role of villain: 'but she would much rather sweep everything under the carpet'.

Liza said nothing, just looked at the floor as if she expected me to tell her off. After some coaxing, she began to defend herself. 'Sometimes Bob loses it about the most stupid things,' she said, 'what's the point of getting wound up about rotating food in the freezer? Life is too short.' Liza was in fact providing something just as important as raising issues: a sense of proportion.

Although I hate sporting metaphors, cricket does help explain the two argument roles in a successful relationship. The person who raises issues is the bowler. The other half who contains issues – or the couple would spend all the time arguing – is the batter. The batter can choose just to block the ball (avoid a row) or hit it for six (and start a row). Although traditionally women might have raised issues and men contained, today the roles are fully interchangeable. Like with cricket, couples can also switch over, so that each partner has an innings of batting and bowling.

Bob and Liza had come into counselling after he had an affair with a work colleague. Naturally, he felt very guilty about how much he'd hurt Liza. He was keen to dig down into his childhood and wondered if he had 'inherited' his unfaithfulness from his father who also had numerous affairs. He also wanted to understand the roots of each and every one of their arguments – which he normally attributed to his infidelity. I knew they were making progress when Liza stopped him: 'Not everything is connected to your affair. I would like to have an argument that was just about' – and she threw out an example – 'whether it's my turn to empty the dishwasher or yours, rather than about your affair. And as for worrying about your father, can't we just concentrate on living our lives?' In effect, Liza had contained their problems.

Both bringing up problems and containing them are equally important. If both partners contain, everything is buried. If both partners bring up problems, so much time is spent analysing that the couple becomes hyper-sensitive and fractious.

'We' and 'I'

Although it is important for couples to spend quality time together, it is equally important for each partner to have time for her or himself. Getting the balance right is hard because it is just as harmful to be too interdependent as too independent.

I have counselled couples who agreed, for example, never to spend a night apart. When they made the vow, it had seemed very romantic. However, by the time they came to my office it had began to feel very claustrophobic.

'I wanted to take my trampoline exams, so I could start to teach,' explained Virginia, forty-five, 'but one of the modules was residential. I knew he'd get moody and, quite frankly, it wasn't worth the aggro.' She hadn't taken the course and had started to resent her husband, Alistair: 'He's holding me back and stopping me from being myself.' Alistair was prepared for her to go away but thought it was a pity that she didn't want to spend more time as part of the family: 'The kids are still at the age when they want to be with us. It won't last for ever.'

However, in the Intense Learning stage of recovery, each partner begins to take responsibility for their own happiness – rather than just blaming the other. Certainly, this is what happened with Virginia and Alistair. 'I realised it's not up to Alistair to make me happy,' said Virginia, 'I've got to do that for myself. I could stand up for what I need rather than keeping quiet and being resentful – because that's what began to make me feel I *deserved* the happiness I thought I was getting from my lover.' Meanwhile, Alistair had begun to think about his own needs and not just the couple's needs: 'There're things I want to do – like go to a Grand Prix – which don't interest either my wife or my daughters.' They had begun to balance the 'I' and the 'we'.

In most cases, couples who are too independent – and have forgotten the 'we' in their relationship – have already recognised the need to spend more time together before reaching my offices. So these couples are generally easier to help. If this is you, agree on a regular time to be together – for example, every Wednesday night – and jealously guard it. Otherwise, ferrying the children around, working late or one partner's social activities will sabotage your couple time.

Achieving balance

One of the themes in this book, and indeed in all my writing, is the importance of a balanced relationship. Unfortunately, when couples are in crisis, each partner becomes a more extreme version of themselves. For example, if someone ususally brings up problems, he or she will raise hundreds of them in crisis. Meanwhile, their partner will be containing even more. In fact, the more problems one half brings up, the more the other will feel the need to contain (otherwise it will be problems morning, noon and night) and this will make the other even more anxious and determined to talk (if I don't raise this problem, nothing will ever be solved). Remember how couples can sometimes get stuck on a see-saw argument: the more one half pushes down on her or his end, the higher the other goes up (see page 160). To achieve a more comfortable position, each partner must stop pushing down on their respective end and find balance. For example, once Virginia no longer felt that she needed to guard her personal time so tightly, she was keener on couple time. Conversely, once Alistair stopped guarding couple time, he could recognise the virtue of personal time and his own particular needs.

Looking at achieving balance after infidelity, Jane, forty-five, learnt that there was such a thing as having too high self-esteem: 'I was very complacent and rather arrogant before my husband's affair. I had such a high opinion of myself that if there was a problem – it had to be down to someone else.' In contrast, Alan, forty-one, had very low self-esteem: 'If I felt rejected or not appreciated by Jane, I wouldn't say anything but kept it stored in a dark place inside and used that resentment to justify being unfaithful and my other weaknesses.'

Through counselling, Jane learnt not only to show her approval and but also how much she valued Alan. Meanwhile, Alan learnt that being selfish did not help him feel better about himself: 'I needed to grow some balls and stand-up for myself.' Jane thought for a moment and concluded: 'I've stopped hiding behind my "I'm perfect" front and become, I suppose, more human.' They had achieved a more balanced relationship without the extremes of high and low self-esteem.

Returning to Robert and Rosie, the child-centred couple from the previous chapter, their relationship became more balanced too during the Intense Learning stage: 'When we got married, it was like a fairy-tale come true,' said Rosie, 'he was rescuing me from my parents who argued like cat and dog. I felt like Cinderella.' That, of course, made Robert into Prince Charming – someone who had to carry the load of always being perfect. They had got married when Rosie was nineteen and in many ways he had always been 'in charge'. The couple decided it was time to have a more balanced relationship and set time aside every evening to listen to each other's daily concerns. By taking on her share of responsibility for what went wrong, Rosie no longer felt like a little girl – at the mercy of Robert's behaviour – and more in charge of her own life.

The three fundamentals of a good sex life

Having covered the qualities that make someone less vulnerable to having an affair for legitimacy reasons, we move on to the second part of inoculating your relationship by looking at how to guard against seduction. David Blanchflower, the British-born economist from Dartmouth College in New Hampshire, is an expert on data and spreadsheets. However he does not only use this knowledge to predict slumps and forecast the impact of changes in interest rates, he is also interested in predicting happiness and life satisfaction. He has calculated that a good regular sex life is worth £50,000 a year, and it's equally important for men and women. This figure underlines just how vital feeling sexually vibrant is to our overall well-being and conversely just how poor we feel if something is lacking in our love life.

In the eighties, journalist Alexandra Penney's partner was unfaithful and part of her healing process was to interview two hundred men and ask if they had cheated on their partner and why. The top five reasons were as follows:

1. Curiosity
2. Need for variety
3. Sexual frustration
4. Boredom
5. Need for acceptance and recognition

What about women? In the nineties, *Ebony* magazine asked both their readers and therapists for the most common reasons why women cheat. The top five were as follows:

1. A self-esteem boost
2. Emotional neglect
3. Revenge
4. Seeking excitement
5. Seduction and romance

As you might expect, there are marked differences between men and women's reasons for infidelity. However, there is some important overlap. 'Self-esteem boost' is similar to 'need for acceptance and recognition' while 'seeking excitement' is another way of discussing 'boredom'. The seventh most common reason for women cheating is 'sexual deprivation', the parallel problem to men's 'sexual frustration'. So with this research in mind, I have created these three rules:

Allow each other to let off steam
- Talk about celebrities or strangers on the street whom each of you find attractive. Being honest about what turns you on can defuse the fireworks of secret sexual fantasies.
- Tease each other about your passion for Brad Pitt, Angelina Jolie or whoever. This kind of banter allows us to see ourselves and our partners as desirable and passionate people – which is vital for our sexual confidence and overall happiness.
- Allow each other a little mild flirtation at parties. The appreciative glance and the interested laugh is a great

ego boost, plus seeing that other people find your partner attractive can also reignite your own passion for him or her too.

Tell your partner how wonderful he or she is

- Your partner needs to feel that he or she is the best lover in the world. So give lots of feedback – both verbally and physically.
- Give your partner plenty of compliments about his or her body. Even though your partner will probably laugh or disagree. The fact that you appreciate, for example, his or her bottom will increase overall confidence in the bedroom.
- Be proud of your partner's achievements and don't be afraid to voice them. Many people are reticent because they are afraid of gushing or appearing insincere. However, I am not suggesting making things up, just telling your partner your regular private thoughts: 'You work really hard for us and I want to tell you how grateful I am', 'You handled that really well – you're a great father', or 'I know it's taken a toll on you visiting my mother in hospital so often, but I want to tell you that I've been really impressed with your patience.'
- Offer proof of just how wonderful you think your partner is with small acts of appreciation or service. For example, nipping out to buy fresh rolls for her sandwiches or bringing him fresh coffee in bed.
- With your partner feeling both desired and cherished at home, there is no reason why she or he would respond to flattery from someone else.

Let lovemaking become an adventure

- Many people imagine that this involves dressing up, adult toys, bondage and S/M and immediately close their minds to experimentation. If any of these interest you and your partner, that's fine. However, this is not what I'm talking about. The aim is to bring the element of surprise to your lovemaking.

- This can be altering the places where you make love: not just in the bedroom but in the shower, taking a blanket into the woods on a hot summer's evening, or renting a four-poster bed in a country house hotel.
- Being adventurous is being mysterious and never letting your partner know what to expect next. For example, if you have a favourite technique for oral sex use it two times out of three but on the third put in a twist and add something different. For example, what about putting an ice cube in your mouth?
- Look around your house and find other props and tricks to play on each other. What is there in the fridge that you could pour over each other and lick off?
- However, the best aphrodisiac is a turned-on partner, so do not be pressured into doing anything which makes you uncomfortable.
- A partner who is getting loving and adventurous sex will not be tempted by anyone else.

With your overall confidence in the relationship boosted and a more fulfilling sex life in place, it is time to move on to the penultimate ingredient for recovery.

True forgiveness

There is a difference between forgiving your partner enough to try again and the true forgiveness necessary to make infidelity a closed subject. To achieve true forgiveness, there are four ingredients. While the first two are helpful for recovery, it is essential that you embrace the last two:

Reparation

Look at what will repair the damage caused by the affair. Sometimes it might be something practical – replacing the car which had been defiled by illicit lovemaking with the third party, or apologising to your parents for the upset caused. For other couples, it will be something material – jewellery or a romantic trip. If your partner has not made amends, think of something that will help you move forward and tell him or her. Do not expect your partner to be a mind-reader.

Letting go of any anger towards the third party

It is natural to be angry with the other woman or man. However, by this stage in your recovery, it should be possible to look past your first reactions. Alan and Jane were keen to put the affair behind them. They had already taken a four-day trip to Vienna – partly as a celebration of their love surviving and partly as reparation. During this holiday, Jane decided to write a letter to the other woman: 'Not in anger – because there was a time when I wanted to go round to her place and cause a fuss – but to draw a line in the sand and move on.' She read the letter out in counselling and although there was some bitterness – 'Have you any idea what it was like to discover that Alan had brought you to my home and that you'd had sex just inches away from my clothes? I'd call that defilement' – there was also a hint of forgiveness: 'I am aware that you have been hurt too.'

I could understand why she might want to write a letter but less certain about posting it, so Jane explained: 'I wanted her to know that we were back together and doing well, partly so she didn't hang around hoping that we would implode and Alan would come back. Mainly, I wanted to show her that I knew everything as Alan had been completely honest with me and she had no "secrets" that she could hold over me.' The final paragraph of the letter described Jane and Alan's renewed love for each other, an acknowledgement that the other woman had been hurt too and a definite sense of forgiveness. 'Perhaps not just yet, but it's on the horizon,' said Jane.

Putting aside the unhelpful myths about forgiveness

There are many reasons why you might be finding it hard to forgive. Here are just a few myths which make it harder to move on:

- Forgiveness will let my partner off the hook or excuse his or her bad behaviour. (This might have been the case if you had immediately forgiven without going through the previous six steps, but by this point in the journey your partner should have earned forgiveness.)
- My partner might do it all over again. (This myth suggests that punishment is the only way to keep someone faithful. It also places a permanent barrier between you and your partner, and stops healing.)
- He or she does not deserve to be forgiven. (If this is how you feel, you have probably not truly reached Stage Seven. This is also a sign that your partner has not answered all your questions about the affair, so it might be a good idea to re-read Stage Two: Intense Questioning.)
- Forgiving means forgetting and I could never do that. (The memories will remain but forgiving takes away their continued power to hurt.)
- I can only forgive if certain conditions are met – for example, a full apology is given. (There is more about apologies in the box for the Discovered at the end of this chapter.)
- People will criticise me if I forgive. (I have two thoughts for you. First, have you kept your family and friends abreast of your progress or do they still picture you at the beginning of the journey? How could you update them? Second, you cannot please everyone.)

After having looked at what forgiveness is *not* about, it is time to focus on what it really means. If forgiveness is truly given – and not coerced – it allows us to let go of resentment, blame and anger. Therefore, *forgiveness is not just an act of generosity to our partner but also a gift to ourselves.* This is because it frees us from the past, allows us to draw a line and to start afresh. Finally, forgiving our partner makes it easier to forgive ourselves too.

Identifying the lessons and the gifts

At the beginning of this book, I talked about the danger and the opportunity in the crisis of infidelity. The opportunity is to learn some important lessons (something that can be applied in the future) and to gain some useful gifts (new perspectives or greater wisdom). If you are still finding it hard to reach true forgiveness, looking at your lessons and gifts will help.

When Judy, forty-five, discovered her husband's two-year affair, with a woman whose children went to the same school as their own, she was furious. Particularly as they had already been in marital therapy for a year. She even started looking at revenge websites. Fortunately, she found my book (*I Love You But I'm Not in Love with You*), read it in five hours and decided that there should be a way to make things better. She also filled in my 'Infidelity in the UK' survey and identified the following learning about herself: 'I should have been more open, told my husband that I disliked certain things, argued more with him – and because I didn't do that enough I was angry a lot of the time and, therefore, couldn't give him intimacy any more.' With this story in mind, what have you learnt, what gifts (however unwanted) have you received, and what more learning could you do?

The majority of people in my survey learnt something positive from infidelity. The most common lesson – 25 per cent of the sample – was 'I'm stronger'. To reflect the spread of opinions, I have grouped the responses into four categories:

Positive personal lessons

Fifty-five per cent were upbeat. After 'I'm stronger', the most common lessons were: 'I can forgive' and 'I need to be myself'. Other positive lessons included: 'I am not a victim' and 'It's okay to be sad and cross but don't let it ruin your day'.

Negative personal lessons
These responses made up 18 per cent and underline how painful infidelity can be. The most common reply was 'I'm stupid' (7 per cent of the total sample), followed by 'I lack confidence'. Other examples include: 'Although I thought I was strong and happy, I am a weak and lonely woman', 'My capacity to forgive is huge but to forget is minute and my ability to keep up appearances is remarkable' and 'I can bury my head in the sand and jog along'.

Aspirations for the future
This group comprised 15 per cent of the sample. The most common replies were 'I need to confront more' and 'I must work harder at my marriage'. Other examples include: 'I need to be more open to more people and speak more of my emotions. I was like Mr Spock, very little emotion would seep out of me'.

Lessons about marriage and life in general
The final category has 12 per cent of people in it. The most common lesson was about the importance and reliability of friends. Others include: 'Marriage is the most important thing', 'I can't sort out my partner's life for him', and the value of 'honesty, fairness and truthfulness'. One of the most interesting replies came from someone who had been unfaithful: 'I am happy with my lot in life and don't need to be chasing after rainbows or the grass-is-greener scenario and how many people can honestly say that?'

How to trust again

As this book is called *How Can I Ever Trust You Again?*, there should be a long section on how to regain trust. However, over the past three stages, some key elements of your recovery have been put in place. During Stage Four (Hope), your partner will have offered or agreed to be more transparent about his or her movements. Your partner should have cut off all contact with

the third party and shown a commitment to put that relationship behind her or him by answering all your questions about
the affair. During Stage Five (Attempted Normality), communication between the two of you should have improved. During
Stage Six (Despair – Bodies Float to the Surface), your partner
has shown a commitment to settle long-running disputes and
lay the foundations for a renewed relationship. Finally, in this
stage, you have begun to focus on temptation and to inoculate
your relationship against future sexual problems.

Under these circumstances, trust should fall automatically into
place. Often it happens so quietly that many people only realise
after the fact. Perhaps their partner is late home and they are busy
and don't notice the time. It is only later that they register the
absence of the clenched gut or racing mind.

How can you tell when you've begun to trust again? The best
indicator that the crisis is over is when the two of you can start
planning or dreaming about the future together. Previously,
these thoughts will have been fantasy and part of your private
daydreams. Once trust has returned, ideas are openly discussed
and there are concrete plans for a future together.

What if all the ingredients of trust are in place but something
is holding you back? 'I want to trust and Lyle has been quite
sweet; he's given me his password and I can read his emails and
check his phone,' says Candice, twenty-eight, 'and he seems
genuinely sorry. I believe the affair is over but I can't let go.
I keep on and on at Lyle and I'm worried that it's driving us
apart.' So I suggested that Candice tried an alternative strategy
for two weeks. I call this strategy 'Act as if'. Instead of worrying
that he might be unfaithful, she had to think: 'What would I do
if I trusted him?' And then follow up by turning this imagined
behaviour into reality. The experiment was an almost immediate
success. The temperature in their household lowered. Lyle was
more open – he no longer expected to be attacked at any moment
– and they grew much closer. Before too long, Candice did not
need to 'act as if' she trusted because she really did.

For the Discovered: Intense Learning

- This is the final stage in the healing process. Your relationship is much stronger but to reach recovery, there is one final ingredient.

- It will probably feel like you have done nothing but say 'sorry' since confessing to your affair or being caught out. However, this is not the same as showing true remorse.

- True remorse involves: understanding what you have done; giving a full account of it; acknowledging how you have damaged other people; giving a detailed description of the effects of your behaviour; expressing regret and putting forward a proposal to make amends.

- Anything less will seem, to your partner, like an attempt to wriggle out of the consequences of your infidelity or to fake remorse.

- For this reason, it is only at the end of the journey that you will have enough knowledge about yourself and your relationship to be able to apologise properly.

- The five necessities for a fulsome apology are: Acknowledge what you did wrong. (For example, 'I have cheated and lied not only to you but to the children.') Accept your responsibility for the inappropriate behaviour – without explaining the background, as this can seem like excusing it. ('I was selfish and thought only about myself.') Hold yourself responsible for the consequences. ('I have hurt you and by not taking proper precautions put your sexual health at risk.') Express sorrow. ('I am truly sorry and ashamed.') Explain why it will never happen again. ('I am determined that I will not make the same mistakes again and, for example, I have resolved to come home early on Friday nights rather than socialising with my work colleagues.')

> - A fulsome apology will allow your partner to forgive and finally move on.
>
> - If affairs start when: Problem + Poor Communication + Temptation = Infidelity, what have you learnt about settling future disputes between you and your partner? How has your communication improved for the better? How could you head off temptation in the future? Share your discoveries with your partner.

New skill: Continuous development

Returning to the three fundamental beliefs outlined in the first chapter, which are destroyed by discovering infidelity, how do they look now?

1. The world is meaningful.
2. I am worthy.
3. The world is benevolent.

During this Intense Learning stage, you have looked at just how much you have learnt (however unwillingly) from the affair. In this way, you have begun to find something meaningful from your experiences and a way of imposing meaning on the world. During the journey from discovery to recovery, your self-esteem has been at least partially restored. Just by surviving infidelity, you will have discovered reserves of strength and a depth of feeling of which you were probably not aware. You are well on the way to feeling worthy again. The final fundamental belief – the world is benevolent – is harder to reconcile. We want to think that life is good but we know that there are wars, natural disasters and that people die. As we get older, we have a choice: either we accept that the black-and-white ideas of our childhood need updating or we can block our ears to the truth and sing 'la, la, la'. I believe that accepting that life is both good and bad makes us appreciate the benevolent parts more, and feel less personally affronted when we get our share of the malevolent. Ultimately this makes for a better and more fulfilled life.

Moving on to the particular skill from this stage, continuous development is about growth – for ourselves and our relationship. We want to believe that when Elizabeth marries Mr Darcy in *Pride and Prejudice*, when Maria and Baron Von Trapp climb over the mountains at the end of *The Sound of Music,* and Hugh Grant declares his love for Julia Roberts in *Notting Hill*, their lives are frozen in happiness – but this is not the whole story. Relationships are living things and cannot stand still. They need continuous development or they risk becoming stale, and possibly withering and dying. This final skill, to keep renewing your relationship, might seem like an effort – and a far cry from a fairy-tale ending – but actually it turns love into an adventure and the most precious gift of all.

Summary

- The two main reasons for people being unfaithful have been addressed – legitimacy and seduction – and the couple have learnt enough so that these are unlikely to be issues again in the future.
- All the problems and uncertainty that were thrown up by discovery have been settled and the world is beginning to look better again.
- The partner who has been unfaithful has made a fulsome and informed apology. Their other half has offered forgiveness.
- Forgiveness is the best way to take the pain out of the past and to move on. In this way, it is the best gift that you can give yourself.
- By this point you are not certain how, but you have started to trust your partner again.

Exercises

What do I admire about my partner?

If 'being taken for granted' is one of the most common reasons given for adultery, this exercise is the complete opposite. It aims to pinpoint everything that you value about your partner but has somehow fallen beneath your conscious radar.

So take a piece of paper and write the following headings down one side and then return and put something beside each one. Don't give it too much thought, just put the first thing that comes into your head. If you draw a blank, skip that heading and keep going. Afterwards, come back and fill in the blanks. The more headings that you can write something beside, the better.

So what do you admire about your partner?

1. Character
2. At work
3. As a parent or in relation to children
4. Talent
5. Around the house
6. Around the garden
7. Appearance
8. As a friend
9. Practical matters
10. Emotional matters
11. Attitude to parents
12. Socialising
13. In the wider community or neighbourhood
14. Cooking
15. Sport
16. Hobbies
17. Pets
18. Money
19. In adversity
20. Spirituality

If you are working through this book with your partner, you might like to both do this exercise and then show each other the results. Alternatively, use your findings so that you can tell your partner how great he or she is.

Playing devil's advocate

This exercise is designed to help you break out of the rut of repeating the same row over and over again.

1. Instead of arguing your own viewpoint, take your partner's side. After all, you've heard it often enough.
2. Meanwhile, your partner takes your side and argues your case as strongly as possible.
3. Allow the argument to follow its normal course.
4. Don't worry if you start to laugh or muck around. There probably is something ridiculous in just how familiar this argument has become.
5. Afterwards, discuss the experience. What have you learnt from putting your partner's case? What points sounded particularly impressive? What had you got wrong? How have your opinions changed?
6. Bring this new knowledge to the next exercise.

Finding a compromise

Compromise is a skill but with a little knowledge and practice, you can learn to stop fighting and find a solution that works for both you and your partner. There are three steps:

1. Put your preconceptions on hold.
   - Look at your opinions, principles and your preferred solution and ask: How important are they to me and why?
   - What could be holding you back from reaching a compromise? Do you need to win? Do you feel pressurised into agreeing with your partner (so do so grudgingly or later try to sabotage the plan)?

- Are you fighting about matters of principle? This makes it harder to find common ground because you are expecting your partner to have the same principles. The other problem with principles is that they are always based on past experiences and therefore tend to keep you stuck in the past.
- With a better understanding of what drives your side of the argument, commit to change by deciding to enter into negotiations with no preconceptions.

2. Schedule time to talk.
   - Find a time and a place when there will be no interruptions and the children will not be around.
   - Listen to your partner.
   - If your partner is angry or dismissive, it is easy to respond in kind. However, try and concentrate on the message and not the delivery.
   - Afterwards summarise your partner's point. (This is to check that you have not overlaid your own interpretations.)
   - Resist the temptation to comment or attack. This will only encourage your partner to defend her or his opinions and make compromise harder.
   - Change over and take your turn to talk while your partner listens.

3. Look for solutions.
   - You cannot reach a solution until both of you have had your say.
   - Many possible compromises are scuttled because one half comes on too strong too soon and their partner feels pressurised into an early decision.
   - Brainstorm as many ideas as possible, even if some sound ridiculous. Knowing what the two of you don't want can sometimes provide a breakthrough.
   - Look for alternatives beyond you and your partner's favourite options.

- Discuss the consequences of each option and which is best.
- Sometimes a compromise is giving up something that you want, sometimes trading ('If you do "x", I will do "y" . . .'), and sometimes a combination of both.

Checkpoint

Three key points for embracing Stage Seven: Intense Learning

1. Balance your relationship by appreciating your partner's complementary skills.
2. Forgiveness allows you to draw a line in the sand and put the past behind you.
3. The biggest lessons often come from the darkest times.

Diversions, Derailments and Dead-Ends

The good news is that if you work through the seven stages of recovery, about six to nine months later, you will find a deeper, wiser and more fulfilling relationship. Once the first anniversary of discovery has passed, and the two of you have survived birthdays, your wedding anniversary, Christmas and other important dates, you will be ready to close the door on this chapter of your life. On the way, there will be times when you slide back a stage or two – in which case, it is helpful to return and read the last chapter again – but overall progress will be in the right direction. However, certain circumstances will imperil your journey or make it more complicated. This final chapter is dedicated to dealing with these problems. It will cover what to do if your partner is unwilling or unable to recommit to healing your relationship; what to do if your relationship is beyond saving; and how to keep your sanity during difficult times. It ends with an uplifting story.

What if the golden window has passed?

One of my assumptions, writing this book, is that you suspect infidelity or have recently discovered it. In Stage Two: Intense Questioning, I talk about the first six months after discovery as the golden window: the time when your partner is most likely to co-operate. But what if you discovered this book too late? What if your partner refuses to talk because 'it happened ages ago', or 'if you can't let go of the past, there's no hope for the future'?

I have to be honest, the longer after the infidelity, the harder to resolve the problems. Sandra and Jerome had ten great years of marriage until he had an affair. Although they went into counselling, they were unable to resolve anything and the affair hung over their relationship for the next five years. When Jerome formed an inappropriate friendship with one of Sandra's friends, even though she expressly asked him to cut off contact, it brought back all the old feelings. At this point, they separated and came to see me. 'He'd even bought a secret phone so that he could contact her without me knowing,' said Sandra. 'You're doing it again,' said Jerome, 'we can't just relax and spend time together because I know this is all still lurking under the surface and about to rear up and bite me.'

In counselling, we worked on neutralising some of the effects of the first infidelity. However, once we began to look at the inappropriate friendship, Jerome became very angry: 'Is this never going to end?' He turned to Sandra. 'Are you never going to forgive me?' With the couple living apart and spending very little time together, it proved impossible to deal with the layers of mistrust and we ended counselling. So if your partner's affair happened some time ago, what should you do?

First, do not let your resolve weaken. Research from the State University of New York at Stony Brook shows the importance of resolving infidelity. They compared two groups of women with matched levels of marital discord. One group had experienced infidelity, the other had not. However, the women whose partners had been unfaithful were six times more likely to be depressed or anxious.

Second, frame your problems in the 'here and now' rather than keep connecting back to the infidelity. In a sense, you have already been through Shock and Disbelief, Intense Questioning, Decision Time, Hope, and became stuck in Attempted Normality. Unfortunately, it is too late to return to Intense Questioning and address your unanswered questions about the affair. However, you can look at the fundamental issues in your relationship and let the bodies float to the surface. Remember to keep the focus on your life today: 'Why can't we solve any arguments?', 'Why don't we spend more time together?' or 'How can we improve our sex life?' Look back at the exercises in the previous chapter, in particular: Finding a compromise.

What about our children?

Having children together strengthens a couple's resolve to stay together. Unfortunately, children are often drawn into their parents' arguments and start taking sides. When this happens, the healing process can be significantly slowed.

When Catherine, thirty-seven, discovered that her husband Nick, forty-two, had had an affair, she went into overdrive: 'By sheer determination, I kept my marriage on the road. I read all the books and with help from my friends got us all through it. We had to tell our daughters, seventeen and thirteen, because at one point their father was going to leave and set up home with this other woman. They probably guessed there was a problem. I'd lose track of time and they'd come back from school and find me sobbing in the kitchen. I'd pull myself together and cover but they're not blind.'

The couple had come into counselling because Catherine discovered a recent email from Nick to his ex-lover. 'I'd been feeling down and just wondered how she was doing,' Nick said. 'Nothing more. I love Catherine and the girls.'

It soon became clear what was making Nick miserable. Although his wife and younger daughter were willing to forget the past, his older daughter was refusing to talk to him. 'She is very much a daddy's girl and completely heartbroken,' explained Catherine. Even if Nick and his daughter were in the car alone she would not speak, unless to answer a direct question – such as what time she needed picking up. 'I've tried jollying her along but she is very stubborn, so I think it's best to leave it,' Nick said. 'She's like you,' explained Catherine, 'and I worry that if you don't repair the relationship soon, she'll be off to university and it will be too late.'

Nick was definitely someone who contained rather than brought up problems and we spent three weeks on when and how he should tackle his daughter. He was particularly worried that talking might makes things worse: 'At least the house is relatively peaceful at the moment.' However, once he acknowledged his daughter's anger, apologised for the hurt he had caused her and her mother, and stressed how much he loved them both, she forgave him and moved on. Nick and Catherine could finally repair their relationship.

So what should you tell the children? In my opinion, as little as possible. If your children ask questions – because of something that they have heard or observed – confirm that the two of you are having problems, that it is nothing that your children have done, and that you are both working on resolving everything. It is not fair to ask them to keep their mother or father's affair secret. However, be aware that today's children will communicate this information on social networking sites and soon most of your friendship circle and beyond will know.

There are exceptions to my 'little as possible' policy. If your children are likely to hear about their parent's infidelity from outside sources, it is better if the two of you tell them first. What you say will depend on the age of the children. Small children will have no sense of what an affair involves. However, they can understand: 'Mummy or Daddy got too friendly with another man or woman.' Adolescents will be struggling with their own sexuality and the boundaries of what is right and wrong. Their thinking is often very black-and-white, and they are fine-tuned to any sign of hypocrisy. This is why teenagers are the age group most likely to be angry, act out their frustrations, break rules or regress to younger behaviour.

Although it is difficult, because your own problems are currently centre stage, keep a special eye on your children – whatever their age. Look out for unusual behaviour, including acting too grown-up, and be ready to offer extra reassurance. What if your children are older? Can you confide your problems adult-to-adult? I would think very carefully before involving them in your dispute. They will still be hugely impacted by their father's or mother's infidelity. The news can bring up unresolved issues from their childhood or make them fearful for their own relationships.

My partner has been seeing prostitutes

Although prostitution is supposedly the oldest profession, it is only in the last few years that a significant number of couples have sought my help after the husband was discovered paying for sex. Reliable statistics are hard to find but the *Scientific American Mind* magazine estimates that 16 per cent of men in the US have used a prostitute. Meanwhile, a combined study from Imperial College, London, University College, London, the London School of Hygiene and Tropical Medicine, and the National Centre for Social Research has found that the number of men paying for women has doubled from one in twenty to nearly one in ten. There are no figures for women paying men for sex, but anecdotal evidence suggests this is becoming more common too.

The following story from my casebook illustrates the issues involved in infidelity with prostitutes and offers a way forward. When Angie, twenty-eight, found a strange item on her husband's credit-card bill, something in her gut told her to look deeper: 'I presented him with all the evidence and he turned white and admitted to hiring escorts on six different occasions – although I think this is a conservative figure.' Her husband, Duncan, thirty-one, did not disagree. He just nodded and looked sheepish: 'At least there is no emotional involvement and you know I'd never leave you for another woman.'

Like many people caught in the infidelity trap, he had used rationalisation and compartmentalisation to minimise his betrayal. However, for the partners, there are significant differences in uncovering infidelity with prostitutes. The Discoverer is more likely to receive a blow to her or his self-esteem. Indeed, Angie felt 'useless, ugly and inadequate'. There is a greater fear of contracting sexually transmitted diseases and seldom any post-infidelity boost for the couple's sex life. 'I find it hard to relax as I think he's comparing my body to those women,' explained Angie. The final complexity is greater isolation because the Discoverer is normally too ashamed to tell her or his friends.

So what should you do if your partner has been unfaithful with a prostitute? The Shock and Disbelief will be greater and the Intense Questioning stage will be longer. It is important to get some understanding as to why your partner has bought sex. The reasons are normally complex and range from loneliness on business trips and stag parties abroad, through being abused as a child, to sexual addiction. Talking about sex is difficult at the best of times. Unfortunately, your partner is likely to minimise his or her problems through embarrassment and a desire to save you from unsavoury details. However, without full disclosure, it is hard for the Discoverer to make an informed choice about whether to stay in the relationship or not. A relationship counsellor will help you and your partner to talk honestly, keep the conversation focused, and support you both through any painful revelations. If your partner refuses to attend, go on your own and get help for yourself.

In the case of Angie and Duncan, he was able to be honest about the extent of his problem. We explored the part fantasy played in his compulsion to hire prostitutes and the way he used pornography to de-stress from work. Once Duncan learnt better coping mechanisms and reassessed his views about 'nice' girls and sex, he and Angie started to enjoy a fulfilling and satisfying marriage.

My partner is having an affair with someone of the same sex

A surprisingly large number of men and women discover not only that their partners have been unfaithful but also that they are bisexual. According to the 'Social Organisations of Sexuality' study, 3.9 per cent of American men – who are or have been married – had sex with another man in the last five years. That translates into somewhere between 1.7 million and 3.4 million American women who are or were married to men who have sex with men. In the UK, a YouGov Poll had 91 per cent of the population describing themselves as heterosexual, but the figure dropped by 7 per cent when the category 'heterosexual but bi-curious' was added. The ubiquity of Internet pornography and the rise of gay and lesbian dating sites means that more and more people are discovering that their partners have at least 'fantasies' about having sex with someone of the same gender and there is now a new term: mixed orientation marriages.

So what prompts someone with gay or lesbian desires to enter a heterosexual marriage? Although we live in a more tolerant society, many young people still feel inhibited about exploring their sexuality. Add in wishful thinking, ambiguity about their desires, youth, inexperience and an authentic affection for the future spouse, and getting married is not such a giant leap. None of this takes away the feelings of shock on discovering that your husband or wife is not the person that you thought. Worse still, there is a knock-on effect for your own identity and questions about why you were unable to 'satisfy' your partner. If this is your story, what should you do?

The journey from discovery to recovery will follow the same seven steps – even if the shock, shame and isolation are greater. However, from my experience, it is dangerous to minimise your discovery. If your partner says: 'I think I'm gay or lesbian', it is easy to translate this into 'I might not be'. If your partner claims that 'I'm under a lot of stress' and 'this is just a passing phase', these are very seductive claims – as is a straightforward denial that their looking at gay or lesbian pornography means that he or she is attracted to people of the same gender. (It is true that people do not necessarily want to act out all their fantasies. However, the taboo about heterosexual men fancying other men is so strong that it is highly unlikely to be just idle curiosity.)

241

Your partner's feelings cannot be brushed under the carpet – this is what has got him or her and you into this problem in the first place – so spend longer in Intense Questioning and keep returning whenever you have more questions.

If your husband or wife truly is bisexual, gay or lesbian, what does this mean for your relationship in the long-term? The International Straight Spouse Network have found that one third of mixed orientation marriages break up immediately, one third try to resolve the problem but fail, and one third endure. So what makes the difference?

In my experience, the couples who try but fail to rescue their marriage get stuck in Attempted Normality. The women – it is nearly always wives who try and save these relationships – will pretend to trust their man and he will play the dutiful husband (but collect gay pornography or arrange secret gay liaisons). The result is nearly always a second discovery and another round of heartache. However, if couples engage with Stage Six: Despair – Bodies Float to the Surface, and face all the issues, it is possible to maintain a loving relationship. However, in all the cases I have seen, couples come to an arrangement where the man is allowed male sexual partners. Each couple finds a slightly different formula. Some men are allowed only casual pick-ups and others conduct secondary relationships alongside their marriage. Some wives want to know all the details, others would rather be spared. It takes a lot of discussion and a clear sense of what is acceptable and unacceptable. For this reason, it is necessary to keep returning to decision-making – because there is a big difference between what you might tolerate in theory and in practice. However, if a couple have a large reserve of love for each other – and the added incentive of young children – it is possible to sustain a loving and supportive marriage.

Gay relationships and infidelity

Most heterosexuals and lesbians expect their partners to be monogamous. However, gay men often have a completely different take on being 'faithful'. In fact, it can mean everything from being sexually exclusive through to having multiple partners, but being honest about what is going on. Other couples will have a 'don't ask, don't tell' policy and are not too upset if one or both occasionally strays. This breadth of interpretation about what constitutes betrayal can lead to many misunderstandings, confusion and a lot of pain.

'Going into counselling only seemed to fuel our inability to communicate. I thought I was making progress because I was brave enough to risk an argument. However, my partner felt overwhelmed,' wrote Jake, twenty-eight, when responding to my infidelity questionnaire. 'What I didn't know was that he was seeing someone else whom he wanted to be his partner and he wanted me to be his friend. What I also did not see is that we already had an open relationship and he thought it was okay to see other people.' I have to say that you don't discover that you are in an 'open' relationship. This is something that needs to be negotiated in advance. Unfortunately many gay men, like Jake, just assume that their partner has the same take on relationships and get a nasty shock when he crosses their unspoken line. If you have bought this book because of your partner's betrayal, the recovery process will be similar to the seven steps that I've outlined. However, if you are going to regain trust, you will need to discuss the following questions:

- Are you going to be monogamous in the future?
- If not, what degree of outside engagement is acceptable?
- 'One nights' only or is repeat business allowed?
- Are people in your friendship circle off-limits?
- What do you tell each other?
- Can you stay out all night?
- Can you bring people back home?
- What other issues need to put on the table?

What if there has been a baby born from the affair?

During my twenty-five years of counselling couples, I have helped couples where the wife is carrying her lover's baby and where the husband has fathered a child with his lover. If this is your dilemma, the journey will be tougher, more emotional and the stakes will be higher. However, it is still possible for your relationship to survive. So how do you cope?

First and foremost, everything has to be taken in bite-sized chunks. If you try and swallow the enormity of the situation, you will choke. So keep the focus on your relationship: How strong is your bond? How do you feel about each other? Do you love each other? In effect, it is the regular material in the decision-making stage. Put aside the idea of the baby at this point – especially if it is yet to be born. My experience is that you can imagine how you might feel – and probably spend half your waking hours trying to cope with the idea – but the reality will be different. In the meantime, however, you can discover whether the two of you have a strong and loving enough foundation on which to build.

Aaliyah was twenty-five and her husband Jonathan was forty. They had temporarily split when Aaliyah became obsessed with a work colleague. She became pregnant by her lover but their relationship ended and Aaliyah and Jonathan sought my help. Jonathan had been married before and had two teenage children who lived with his first wife. Aaliyah had decided not to tell her former lover about his child: 'It has nothing to do with him. He's completely out of the picture.' Within moments of arriving in my counselling room, they were discussing: What to tell the child when he or she was old enough to understand. Would they be supportive if she or he wanted to trace her or his real father? If the baby was a girl, who would walk her down the aisle on her wedding day?

I had to remind them that Aaliyah was only three months pregnant. So I narrowed the focus down to their immediate concerns: Who should they tell? How did Jonathan feel about family and work colleagues congratulating him on being a father again when he knew he wasn't? Did they want everybody knowing their business? From this discussion, the couple returned the next week with the decision to split people into two categories: 'We're going to tell our families the truth but I can't cope with explaining all the ins and outs to someone I hardly know and bump into at the supermarket,' said Aaliyah. 'We're calling them the A's and B's,' Jonathan joked. However, from this decision, they had come to another conclusion. 'We think it is only right that the child knows the truth,' said Aaliyah. 'We've been talking to a friend who's an adoption social worker and she's told us how they approach the subject.'

I was impressed at how well they were beginning to tackle their problems together and although I had to keep bringing them back to focus on coping with today, they were doing very well. With the immediate dilemmas about the baby solved, we focused on their relationship. What had made Aaliyah unhappy and vulnerable to temptation? Why had they found it hard to communicate properly? In effect, the same issues that every couple face after infidelity. Jonathan and Aaliyah decided that they did love each other and wanted to try and save their marriage.

When a woman is pregnant, there comes a moment when it becomes impossible to continue counselling. The combination of strong emotions, hormones and exhaustion begins to make therapy not only unproductive but needlessly draining. Whatever the background to the pregnancy, I work towards a break at around seven months. So Jonathan and Aaliyah stopped counselling and agreed to start again after the birth. As expected, the situation was completely different when they returned. Jonathan's fears had proved to be groundless and he had bonded with the baby boy: 'I had expected all these complicated feelings. Intellectually, I had known the baby was innocent but it would also be a permanent reminder of a difficult patch in my life. However, all that melted away when I saw him, held him and he became part of my life. I feel like his father.'

It was Aaliyah who was having problems: 'Don't get me wrong, I love my son, but it was only after he arrived that the full enormity of what I'd done hit me.' It took a couple of weeks but once both Aaliyah and Jonathan had expressed their full range of feelings, they were ready for their Intense Learning. During this stage, we discovered that the age gap had made their relationship unequal. So Aaliyah found constructive ways in which to assert herself – rather than the teenage rebellion of the affair – and they left counselling with a stronger relationship.

In many ways, Aaliyah and Jonathan were lucky. The biological father was completely out of the picture. But what if the third party is the mother of the child? This was the situation with Vanessa and George, whom we met in chapter six. His mistress became pregnant in the dying months of the affair and, although George was committed to repairing his marriage, he felt a bond of responsibility to his unborn child and wanted to be part of, as it turned out, her life.

Vanessa discovered that she felt entirely different before and after the birth: 'I had wanted to be compassionate. I didn't mind George seeing this child – although I far from liked it. But the reality was entirely different – it was much, much harder to be magnanimous. My stomach would knot at the idea of him talking to *her*, exchanging emails and still being in contact.' She knew that George was committed to his marriage but doubted the other woman's motives.

In counselling, we spent a lot of time negotiating the access visits. George had to learn to be transparent about the arrangements, particularly when circumstances changed at the last moment – which is often the case with a small baby. Vanessa had to learn to challenge her pessimistic thoughts. For example: 'I will never learn to cope with this,' What was the evidence for 'never'? 'Okay,' she admitted, 'I can't cope at the moment.' Admittedly, Vanessa still felt bleak but she had cut the emotion down to size. She also had to start reporting rather than emoting, so that George understood her feelings but did not feel overwhelmed when he returned from visits.

If this is your problem, here are some basic guidelines:

- Work on removing any remaining secrets. (These bond together the Discovered and the third party.)
- The Discovered should avoid going round to the home of their former affair partner. Face-to-face contact is best kept to public places only.
- The Discoverer will feel powerless and out of the loop. Therefore, the Discovered should volunteer information, however painful or seemingly unimportant. In return, the Discoverer should thank her partner and try and process her feelings before talking the situation over. This stops the Discoverer saying something that will be regretted later, and her partner associating frankness with pain.
- There are only two options, in the long-term, for the relationship between a father and an affair child. First, that he fulfils just his basic financial and legal obligations to the child. Second, that he involves his wife and brings the affair child into his own family – just like he or she was a child from a previous marriage. If the child is not integrated into the marriage, it is not appropriate for the Discovered and the third party to co-parent together.

The final guideline was difficult for George. When Vanessa finally felt strong enough to consider seeing George's daughter, the affair partner refused point blank. I had a one-to-one session with George where he discussed his guilt.

'We had talked about running away and starting a new life together, so I feel like I've let her down.' Did that mean he would be in her debt forever? 'She's on her own, so I feel that I have to tread carefully.' Worse still, he had began to feel bonded to his daughter and worried that if he upset her mother he would not be allowed to see her.

In many ways, he was still in the middle of the affair triangle – trying to keep both women happy. I asked him: 'How do you think Vanessa feels when you defend your affair partner's behaviour?' 'Like I'm still putting her first and Vanessa is number two,' he answered sadly. Ultimately, he had to make a choice. If he wanted his marriage to continue, he had to tell his former mistress that he needed to include Vanessa in the child's life too.

The danger of the 'dry affair'

The alcohol recovery community talk about a 'dry drunk'. These are people who are completely sober but still have the clouded thinking and destructive behaviour of an alcoholic. So a 'dry affair' is when someone is no longer having meaningful contact with the third party but keeps in touch through a mutual friend, web stalking, hoarding souvenirs from the affair, or even seeks to remain 'friends'. The thinking is still clouded because someone in a dry affair minimises the impact of this behaviour on their partner and compartmentalises a special, untouchable place in their heart for their former lover. Dry affairs make it harder, or nigh on impossible, to repair the core relationship and keep couples stranded in Attempted Normality.

Returning to the case of Vanessa and George, he had legitimate reasons for communicating with the mother of his baby daughter. However, he would keep significant developments back from Vanessa. For example, he had exchanged many emails with his former affair partner about setting up a trust fund for their child before even mentioning the idea to Vanessa. 'It's not that I'm against the trust fund,' said Vanessa when he finally told her, 'although we need to think through the implications legally and what it would mean for our children, but I've been completely excluded . . .' She sat in my office unable to finish her sentence. 'You've known that something has been going on but you haven't known what. In some way, it's just like the feelings before you discovered the affair,' I suggested. Vanessa nodded and turned to her husband: 'What message does it give to her? When you're still keeping secrets from your wife?'

It was George's turn to be quiet: 'I suppose she hopes that there is still some chance – which there isn't,' he quickly added. Although George hated the term 'dry affair', he had to admit it described his behaviour. He might have stopped his affair with his work colleague but his relationship with her was not open and transparent.

If a dry affair helps explain what is happening in your relationship, return to Stage Four and look at 'safety-first' living.

What if my partner wants the 'package' but not me?

In most cases, when the affair is discovered, the unfaithful partner's eyes are opened, all the justifications fall away and he or she decides to recommit. However, it is not always so straightforward. There is a significant proportion of unfaithful partners who don't want to leave but are uncertain about staying married. They want the 'package' of home, children and security rather than being 'in love' with their partner. If this is your situation, you have my full sympathy. It is horrible to be seen as just a 'pay packet' or a 'housekeeper'. We all want to be loved for ourselves – not just as a convenient add-on to a comfortable life. Under these circumstances, many people need certainty – 'at least I can get on with my life' – and hope – 'I'm not too old to find someone who will truly love me' – so force their partner to make a decision. However, it is best to understand the background to your partner's indecisiveness before taking action:

Exhausted and indecisive
In high-conflict relationships, where there are countless arguments, the discovery of an affair will be like throwing petrol on flames. The discovered partner becomes frightened of talking about his or her feelings for fear of sparking off another round of recriminations. Therefore, it is tempting to say 'I don't know' – partly because he or she is unsure and partly because it seems

easier. Unfortunately, this makes a difficult situation worse. With no meaningful discussion, the Discovered becomes more and more confused and exhausted from their partner's repeated questions.

Here is a way forward: Take a short break – a weekend or a week away from each other – so you can both recharge your batteries. Afterwards, reassure your partner that you would rather hear the truth – however painful – but change the old patterns by giving yourself twenty-four hours to process his or her answers before responding.

Frightened and indecisive

In low-conflict relationships, where couples swallow their disagreements or ignore them, the discovery of an affair will blast through the seeming tranquillity of everyday life and provide focus. However, once the immediate drama is over, it is easy to settle back into the old routines. The Discovered knows, deep inside, that everything is not right. She or he does not want to hurt their partner again but fears that she or he could be tempted by an affair in the future.

A way forward: You should also read my book, *I Love You But I'm Not in Love with You*, and go back through this book and look at the exercises that deal with better communication.

Overburdened and indecisive

Life would be simpler if our problems came along singly. Unfortunately, infidelity often comes wrapped up with a pack of issues: bereavement, a mid-life crisis, financial problems, a business collapse. Some of these can be the underlying causes behind the affair and others can be sparked by the fall-out from the affair. Whatever the background, the Discovered ends up feeling overburdened and overwhelmed.

A way forward: Pushing for clarity is particularly unnerving for these people who often teeter on the edge of a complete breakdown. So step back and give your partner more time to process everything.

Whether your partner is exhausted, frightened or overburdened, it is important to know that his or her feelings can return and it is possible to fall back in love again. So hold on to this reassurance. Your partner might only want the 'package' at the moment but this is probably a temporary impasse. Make it clear that you want more from your relationship (and are prepared to work for it) but retreat for six months. In the meantime, act in a loving manner, re-read Stages Six and Seven, keep calm and carry on. Once the six months are up, it is time to re-examine both of your feelings and make a more informed choice about the future.

Coping with a yo-yo or unrepentant partner

In the last scenario, the Discovered might have been unclear about what he or she wanted but at least their plans did not involve the affair partner. The worst outcome of all – even more painful than leaving – is where the Discovered shuttles back and forth between their partner and the third party or when they remain in their marriage but are still committed (either emotionally or even physically) to the other person.

Benjamin, forty-one, was found out after being careless with restaurant receipts. He told Sophia, forty, that he wanted time to end his affair properly. She thought seriously about his proposition but asked him to move out. A few weeks later, he was back: 'I missed the kids terribly and the flat I rented was a long way away.' He also made a commitment to his wife and to trying again. However, he still took calls from his mistress while on holiday and went to her rescue when her car broke down. In our session, he finally agreed to end things with his mistress: 'I think she knows that I'm trying to work on my marriage, but I haven't told her in so many words because she gets so terribly upset.' It took him another month to break off all contact but he found it hard to let go: 'If I could flip a switch and turn off my feelings, I would.' During the time we worked together, Benjamin left his wife three times and returned twice. Counselling is not a good forum for decision-making and until he could focus on either one relationship or the other, he was beyond being helped. So I ended our sessions.

Sebastian is forty-six and has been married for twenty years. Two years ago, he discovered that his wife had been unfaithful for two years. They confronted the problems and agreed to work on their marriage for the sake of their teenage children – because 'the shock and pain to both family and friends would be truly horrific'.

A year later, Sebastian found a secret second phone and confronted his wife. He wrote in my survey into infidelity: 'She was strangely calm and claimed to have got rid of it. This is not the case and I have proof that they are still carrying on. It's one thing to know about the initial two years but worse to know that it is still going on under my nose – despite my best intentions. There are times when I'm hopeful. A simple smile like the old days. A thank-you or a family joke around the dinner table feels like an induced high; afterwards, I'm extremely tired and for once can get a good night's sleep.' Sebastian feels trapped: 'Nobody is aware of the situation and the depth of betrayal because I do not want to upset the children. My wife leads a double life and I am in a living nightmare. The person I met all those years ago died but, without a tangible end to our marriage, I can't move forward myself. I am unable to say goodbye or grieve over what I have lost. On a positive, I think my relationship with the children has improved and I've learnt a depth of feeling that I was unaware of. I must try and balance my life more.'

In order to deal with these types of scenarios, it is important to understand the power and the durability of a triangle. As previously discussed in Stage Three, engineers use triangles in large construction projects – like bridges – because they can safely carry heavy loads. In contrast, a simple girder would buckle under the same weight. And this is the key to breaking free. Instead of hoping, begging or issuing ultimatums for your partner to change, you need to walk away. Okay, in the short term, he or she will probably run into the arms of his or her affair partner but as you will read in the next scenario, this is unlikely to lead to happy-ever after. Once the triangle is broken, the affair relation-ship is taking all the strain and for the first time is truly tested. However, more importantly, walking away will begin to restore your peace of mind and self-respect. Then, if your partner does return, rather than letting him or her back with nothing more than a promise to try harder, you will be strong enough to lay down conditions: no future contact with the affair partner, going into therapy and whatever else will aid your recovery.

What if my partner leaves me for his or her lover?

At first sight, everything might seem cut and dried. Your partner has met the 'new' love of his or her life. They are 'soul partners' and have walked hand-in-hand into the sunset. However, do not assume that they will be happy together. As a marital thera-pist, I get to see what happens next. A typical example would be Rosemary, in her late forties, and Luke, in his late thirties. The last five years truly had been a roller-coaster. Rosemary's husband had discovered her infidelity two years into the affair and she had promised to end it. 'I really did try,' she explained in my office, 'but I just could not give up Luke.' She tried to squeeze his knee, to show how important their relationship was to her, but Luke just turned away. It was clear that he was very angry. 'I was completely obsessed with Rosemary, I couldn't sleep, I couldn't eat. I couldn't live with the idea that he [her husband] was touching her,' he explained.

Eventually, the affair came to light for a second time. 'My husband still wanted to save the relationship,' said Rosemary, 'but it was just impossible. Anyway, that's all in the past and there's so much to look forward to . . .' Her voice trailed away as she looked at the grim expression on Luke's face. 'I thought that once the divorce had come through, which was bitter and protracted, we'd be out of the woods,' she continued, but Luke interrupted: 'You just don't get it, do you?' The frustration and bitterness was written all over his face. So what had gone wrong?

When an affair stops being secret and becomes public, two things happen. First, some of the excitement drains away from the relationship. Humans are contrary creatures. Once we have permission and the opportunity to have sex as often as we wish, the desire tends to decrease quite significantly. In addition, while forbidden sex is automatically thrilling, lusty and pleasurable, lovemaking in a long-term relationship needs good communication, consideration and practised technique. As most affairs are built on passion, this change can be very destabilising.

However, the second factor is far more important: the affair partner is so desperate for a full-time relationship that he or she will swallow their own needs, forgive almost anything and still keep a smile on his or her face. Even in the short term, this is difficult to sustain. In the long-term, it is impossible. Luke's resentment centred around a holiday that Rosemary's husband booked to the Maldives. 'I went as a "friend",' she explained, 'after all I'd put him through, it was the least that I could do.' 'He was trying to get you back,' Luke replied. 'Okay, okay. He might have done. But I made it perfectly clear beforehand that was not going to happen,' said Rosemary. 'How do you think I felt for those two weeks?' Luke shot back. 'It was a mistake, I accept that now,' Rosemary acknowledged.

Rosemary tried to be conciliatory but it made little impact on Luke. It soon became clear that this holiday was just the most extreme example of how Rosemary had tried to keep both men happy but had ultimately just enraged them both. Unfortunately, Luke had been so busy playing the perfect understanding lover that Rosemary had not realised the full extent of his misery. Worse still, while Luke had been determined to win Rosemary, he had convinced himself that he did not want children. Now he had Rosemary, he was beginning to question this decision. It was like a dark version of the Stage Six: Despair – Bodies Float to the Surface.

I tried to counsel them for a couple of weeks but without success. While most relationships have a solid beginning, which is a resource when times become hard, this one had been built on deception and therefore had no reliable foundations. 'I just can't trust her or anything that she says,' explained Luke when they ended counselling. 'She's lied to me just too many times.' It was strange to hear the third party speaking the same lines as the partner who discovers an affair.

The odds might be in favour of your partner's new relationship imploding but that does not mean that he or she will automatically return. So if you still want to save your relationship – despite everything that has happened – what do you do?

Take a reality check
It is important to assess the strength of your relationship's foundations. The following questions will help. As an example, I have put in the answers from an enquiry to my website and my concerns about her answers:

- How long have you been together? (In this case: three and a half years.) I am always concerned when a couple have been together for less than four years. This is because 'limerence', the walking-on-air feeling when two people fall in love, lasts for somewhere between eighteen months and three years. During this early courtship, the attraction is incredibly strong – almost like a chemical reaction. At its height, a couple want to spend every waking minute together and if this is not possible will dream about or talk to friends about their beloved. During limerence, it is almost impossible to believe that there is anybody else in the world beyond your beloved – let alone think about having a relationship. Once limerence subsides – which is inevitable – the real work of forming a relationship begins. Unfortunately, many people think that as the limerence wears off they have fallen out of love and perhaps start looking around for other people with whom to repeat the high again.
- What are the ties between you and your partner? (In this case: 'We had plans for marriage, names for future kids,

future housing . . .) Unfortunately, the ties can be based on your belief in how things could be – rather than the solid reality of how things have been. The couples who have the greatest chance of reuniting after a separation caused by an affair have children and shared property.

- What are the obstacles to getting back together? (In this case: 'I miss his companionship because he was like my only family, because I was kicked out of home and stayed at different rental places because my parents didn't like him for the religious influence he exerted over me. He is a Muslim and I'm a Chinese Christian, but I was willing to convert.') Be honest about your own obstacles. What chance do you have of overcoming them?

- What supports do you have? (In this case: 'I've few friends because he was my best friend and it's been terribly lonely without him talking to me now. I feel so helpless.') It is important to be aware that you are embarking on a hard journey and it is tougher still if you do not have someone offering practical and emotional support.

Remember that it takes two people to make a good relationship
In many relationships where one person has been responsible for all the 'we' moments, the other partner is free to concentrate on all the 'I' time. This sort of polarisation can seriously undermine the self-confidence of the partner fighting to save the relationship; he or she ends up feeling unattractive and never quite good enough. So what happens if this person stops texting, calling and arranging outings? Either the relationship collapses – it takes two people to make a relationship – or the second partner steps into the gap and starts to call or arrange something themselves.

The other advantage of stopping calling, even for a few days, is the chance for thoughtful reflection. Many people fighting to save a relationship set small goals: 'If I can persuade him to meet for coffee on Wednesday' or 'If I can get her to put off moving into the spare room'. They become so obsessed with making these dreams into a reality, that they lose sight of the bigger picture.

Worse still, they read deep and meaningful intentions into their partner's behaviour when, in reality, a coffee is just a coffee and staying in the bedroom is only to keep the peace – not a declaration of love. However, when there are no immediate goals on the horizon, the partner trying to save the relationship can look at the other's overall behaviour – not just selected snapshots – and make a more thoughtful diagnosis.

Do not close down other options

Although it is unwise to rush headlong into a new relationship, job or move to the other end of the country during a personal crisis, it is important to be open to new experiences. So if a friend suggests going away on a spa break, walking the Pennine Way or doing an Adult Education course together, take up the offer. It is much better to be out circulating than leaving chunks of free time on the off-chance that your partner might call. I would also accept 'dates' too, as new people will bring possible new interests into your life and a chance to experiment with being single again.

The tasks of moving on

Although infidelity is painful, it is possible to recover, renew the loving bond and discover a better relationship than before. However, I am a realist. Some relationships have been heading downhill for so long that all the goodwill is exhausted; the only realistic option is to learn from it and move on. If you recognised that your partner was a Don Juan (or Doña Juana) or had had an Exit affair, it is often better to heal alone.

1. Ending the relationship

If deciding to leave a relationship is hard, sticking to that decision is even harder. For every bad time, there is probably a good time to remember. In addition, there is plenty of remorse: what if we had . . . (fill in with your particular regret) and if only . . . (fill in with your particular hope). The whole situation is made more complicated because the minute one partner makes up his or her mind to leave, the other will immediately shift from confused to determined to save the relationship. The result is that the whole 'shall I stay or shall I go' debate is reopened. However, there comes a time when considering all the options, and keeping an open mind, becomes just torturing yourself. This is especially the case when second chances have become third, fourth or even fifth chances. (If you are still not certain, look at the exercise at the end of this chapter: Shall we give our love another try?)

Lauren and Adam had been together on and off for seven years. Their relationship had started as an affair during the slow disintegration of Adam's marriage and, although he had divorced three years previously, Lauren and Adam's relationship was still mired in the past. Lauren was angry and Adam was defensive. Worse still, they had started pushing, shoving and hitting each other.

'If only he'd leave me alone, I could get on with my life,' complained Lauren. 'I will do, but you keep calling me up: "There's a problem with my car",' Adam countered. 'I'll help out and we'll get talking or have sex.' As if by magic, the relationship would be back on again. However, nothing fundamental had changed. A few weeks, or even a few hours, later and the same old arguments would launch them back into the same old cycle.

Eventually, I was able to help them understand how destructive their relationship had become and truly end the relationship. They both felt a huge sense of relief. 'I didn't realise how much stress I'd been under until it was over,' explained Lauren. 'We both know where we stand and that's much easier,' added Adam.

2. Being civilised

Every couple who splits starts off promising to 'stay friends'. However, this requires the best of instincts at the worst of times. So how do you get over this hurdle? My golden rule for making any relationship work becomes even more important when a couple is splitting up but wants to remain civilised: *Treat your partner as you would wish to be treated yourself.* If you are considerate, the odds are that your partner will be considerate too. If you try to punish, get revenge or start playing the martyr, it is almost certain that your partner will respond in a similarly unhelpful manner. The spiral of attack and counter-attack means the break-up soon slips from civilised to bitter to toxic.

So how do you avoid this trap? It is important to understand how the decision to split will dramatically change your perspective, so be ready to compensate. Martha and Clive, in their mid-thirties with a young child, came for counselling to either save or end their relationship. In the first set of sessions, when we tried to find a future together, Clive was full of indecision: 'I don't know' or 'I'm confused'. Although Martha would get exasperated, she generally kept it under control. After a particularly painful and stuck weekend, when the couple seemed further apart than ever, they arrived at our counselling session with a decision. Martha explained: 'We want to part on good terms and, as we're still friends, this seems like the best time to leave.' Clive agreed: 'Otherwise we could start hating each other and that's not good for our daughter.' So we moved into the second phase and started to discuss the issues raised by separation. Clive remained indecisive and uncertain about his feelings. However, Martha's reaction changed completely. Instead of exasperated, she became bitter. Instead of being friends, they started to trade insults. Within the space of one session, and much to my surprise, they had turned from friends to enemies. So what happened?

A relationship – even one in crisis – has a protective layer. In general, each partner will hope for the best and interpret the other's behaviour in a reasonably positive or at least neutral light. Once a couple decide to part, each partner fears the other will become vengeful or vindictive and quickly finds evidence to back up his or her negative expectations. Once Martha had replaced her rose-tinted glasses with a negative magnifying glass, a statement like 'I don't know', which before the split was interpreted as 'He could want us to stay together' became 'He can't even give me a straight answer' after the split. In the same way, 'I'm confused' turned from a description of his state of mind into something completely negative: 'He's hiding something'. No wonder their relationship deteriorated so quickly.

3. Mourning the loss

The end of the relationship is like a bereavement. Even if there is something to celebrate – like escaping a partner who was disrespectful, abusive or undermined your self-confidence – there are still lost dreams and dashed hopes. These need to be acknowledged and mourned. However, our culture finds loss and disappointment difficult to express and when we are in pain there is the natural desire to move on as quickly as possible. Unfortunately, this just makes matters worse. So instead of dulling the pain with drink, shopping or prescription drugs, take time to understand what went wrong and recuperate. (Look at the exercise 'Mourning the loss' on page 204.)

4. Reclaiming yourself

At the beginning of a relationship, a couple have to transform themselves from two separate individuals into one partnership. To this end, couples pool their talents and one partner, for example, cooks while the other fixes things around the house. On a deeper level, one person might look at a problem rationally while the other looks at the emotions. This team building means that we invest our partner with special talents: you are good with money or you are brilliant at solving disputes between the kids. Often we deliberately forget some skills – to make our partner feel wanted or special – or lose them through neglect.

So make a list of all the tasks that were the responsibility of your ex-partner and one that covers everything that you did. Look at your list first, and remember that you are a resourceful and talented person. Second, look at your partner's list. What did you do before you met him or her? What skills could you rediscover?

If there are truly black spots on the list – for example, fixing the car – where could you find someone to perform the task for money or as a favour?

5. Experimenting

Ending a relationship is sad but it brings the possibility of new adventures. Instead of being depressed about the blank spaces in your diary – that used to be filled by couple time – look at the opportunity of doing something new. Ask yourself: what interest have I never followed because my ex-partner would have felt excluded or simply because of lack of time?

Tiffany, forty-nine, had always wanted to explore her love of singing. 'My husband's full-on career had meant that free time for us as a couple was not only limited but unpredictable, so I found it hard to commit to anything regular. That all changed when we split, my time became much more my own. Our eldest son was at university and our daughter had passed her driving test, so I joined a choir. I not only enjoyed the singing but also found the social side equally rewarding.' Clubs and social activities are good places to meet people. They are also not particularly couple-orientated and provide an opportunity to fly solo in social situations again.

What about experimenting with a new relationship? Although someone finding you attractive can boost your self-confidence, it is unwise to rush straight into a new relationship. Not only does this risk bringing all the old baggage into the new relationship, but you are also going through a period of great change and learning about yourself. What seems right at the moment might not be such a perfect fit in six months' time. However, a few dates and a mini-relationship – that concentrates on having fun together – can be a good way of discovering what works and what doesn't work for you. There's more advice about being newly single in my book *The Single Trap: The Two-Step Guide to Escaping It and Finding Lasting Love*.

A positive ending

If your relationship has been irreparably broken, it can seem impossible that anything good will come out of the experience. However, the following case history shows how pain can be a springboard into a better future.

Rosalie first discovered her husband-to-be was unfaithful after only a year of dating. 'I was devastated and after I confronted him, caught a flight to Holland to stay with my father and brother. He went round to my mother's and although he had never met her begged her to tell him where I was. He flew out to Holland and found me. He knocked on the door, I opened it, and was shocked to see him. He told me for the first time that he loved me and everything else that I wanted to hear. I was completely flattered that anyone would "love" me enough to make such a gesture.'

They started living together and married four years later. 'Over our seventeen years together, I got to read the signs that he was lying. His face would slightly change and his body language was different. He was a session musician and toured with bands all over the world. I would go through his wallet when he got home, looking for any phone numbers, receipts or signs that he was spending money on other women and every time I found them. One day I received a large package sent by the management company of the pop star he was on tour with. It was filled with hundreds of love letters to him, each one had a story of a relationship with him. Some begged him to leave me and live with them, others went into graphic detail of the sex they had had. One girl even sent gifts to our small children. Sometimes I got anonymous letters and phone calls. Other times a friend would call round and tell me what he was up to. Once my brother saw him with another woman who was pushing my son along in a pram – I was at work at the time. Each time I forgave him, I was hurt beyond repair and it almost destroyed me.'

Rosalie and her husband settled into a pattern. 'I would find out about his latest affair and cause a drama by going to her house. If I found out after it had happened, then I would shout at him and he'd be deeply ashamed and beg forgiveness. I would give him the cold shoulder for a few days and he'd buy me a piece of jewellery or take me away for a weekend. I would forgive him, feeling lucky that we were still together.' The end of the marriage took a long time coming. 'I was done with forgiving him but I wanted a miracle to stop me from wanting a divorce. I was committed to this man but he did everything he could to destroy my self-image. Finally, I was at the bottom of my reserves, with nothing left to give, and I was not going to let my children suffer from my weakness. They helped me make the decision as they slept in their beds – [they were aged] five and nine. After he left, I had space to think about what I really wanted. There were times when I was tempted to give it another go. However, I had a call from a friend: My brother's wife had left him and moved in with my husband! There it was, the last nail in the coffin of my marriage. Had the affair been going on under my nose? I didn't care any more and was strangely relieved: it was over.'

However, Rosalie's story has a happy ending. 'Three months after he left, I went back to school. I gained three A-levels and went on to do a degree, the first in my family. Today, I'm forty-eight and head up a department of a multinational company. Not bad for someone who was so lacking in self-confidence that, at one point, I needed tranquillisers to leave the house.'

I have one final piece of information to make you feel optimistic. Although you might feel overburdened with baggage, it is generally easier for divorced people to find love than someone who has never been in a long-term relationship. Especially as, if you had several happy years with your partner, you have learnt important relationship skills. With time and a little work, you *will* be ready to love again.

For the Discovered: Diversions, Derailments and Dead-Ends

- If you have been unable to give up your affair partner, or continued contact behind your partner's back, the recovery process will have been slower or have stalled altogether.

- If you have realised your mistake and wish to try again, it is important to put yourself into your partner's shoes and understand the depth of the betrayal.

- If you are still having a 'dry affair' – a term from Alcoholics Anonymous to describe someone who is sober but still living destructively – it is important to stop feeding your old feelings by remaining 'friends' with your ex-lover. Most dry affairs happen at work where there is still professional if not meaningful contact. So using another AA term: if you are in danger of slipping, don't go to slippery places. Find ways of removing even the smallest interactions with your ex and fill the hole in your life with new hobbies, exercise, improving your mind or rebuilding bridges with your partner and family.

- It will take time to woo your partner again and earn the chance to try again. Do not expect too much too soon.

- Think about the changes you need to make for your relationship to work this time round. Commit to making these changes and keep them up for a sustained period – even if your partner is uncertain about a future together.

- Listen to your partner's hurt without interruptions, explanations, pleas for clemency or protestations about future fidelity. Ask questions so that you really understand his or her hurt and afterwards acknowledge the depth of pain that you have caused.

- If you can demonstrate change, the ability to truly listen and be patient, it is possible to return to the Hope stage and complete the journey from discovery to recovery.

New skill: Understanding the difference between closure and transcendence

When I first started counselling couples in the eighties, my clients never spoke of 'closure'. However, over the years, the term has become commonplace. So what's brought about the change? Perhaps we hope by understanding exactly what happened and why, or making some dramatic gesture (such as confronting the third party or burning our partner's clothes), that we can package up the past and its power to hurt us. My concern is that many people seeking 'closure' are hoping for a quick route out of their pain. They only want to learn the most superficial lessons (often about their partner rather than themselves) and skip the mourning phase of recovery all together. I also wonder if 'closure' is actually possible. Especially as, when two people have shared many experiences together – and have children – it is wrong to try and deny this history. Surely the goal should be to integrate the past into a different future?

What about 'closure' and infidelity? Closure seems to suggest wiping the slate clean and starting again and, therefore, is very seductive. But although it is possible, and desirable, to forgive your partner – should you forget? Probably not. Forgetting suggests moving on without learning or holding your partner to account if he or she is unfaithful again. This is why the ultimate goal should be transcendence. This term has a religious background and means 'going beyond' or 'rising above'.

If you can run into your partner's lover and, instead of being consumed with anger, feel largely indifferent, or, instead of being obsessed with what she or he is wearing or doing, you are only mildly interested, this is proof that you have truly moved on. The pain might still be there but you can rise above it. At last, you have reached transcendence and my job is done.

Summary

- Most couples will slip back, from time to time, on the road to recovery but some issues – like children becoming involved in their parents' dispute and taking sides – can cause a derailment.

- The longer after discovery that a couple waits to start to work on their relationship, the harder it is to recover.
- If your partner has ended contact with the third party but is not still fully committed to your relationship again, this is a handicap but not a barrier to healing.
- If your partner is yo-yoing back and forth between you and his or her affair partner, remember it takes three people to make a triangle – and you don't have to be one of them.
- Even if your partner leaves, this doesn't prevent you from reaching recovery. The seven steps still stand but the final stage is focused on learning about yourself, what you need in the future and how to heal alone.

Exercises

Shall we give our love another try?

If your partner bailed out when bodies started to float to the surface or disappeared with the third party before you had a chance to work on the relationship, it is difficult to trust enough to try again. So how should you respond to pleas for another chance?

- Give yourself thinking time. You do not need to respond immediately.
- Imagine what it might be like. Start with how it would feel if he or she first came back. Picture the scene in detail. Next move the camera forward; what would the first week be like? What about a month? What about a year? In each case, try and flesh out each scenario as much as possible. (I would be concerned if your pictures are full of conflict and old problems. I would be equally concerned if you find it impossible to picture a long time into the future.)
- Why would it be different this time? What has changed that will allow the two of you to complete the recovery journey? The absence of the third party alone is not enough.
- What is your bottom line? Everybody has some basics on which it is impossible to compromise. I had one client who insisted that her husband should return to their bedroom and not the spare bed. I would suggest insisting on a 'safety-first' policy, too. Think about what you need. Don't keep these issues to yourself, negotiate with your partner and discover his or her bottom line.
- What are the negatives? There are several important contra-indications to consider. Is your partner domineering, controlling or manipulative? Can you talk openly and honestly? Does your partner have a serious drink, drug or gambling problem? Are you considering trying again on the back of passionate sex? It is incredibly common for separated or even divorcing couples to have hot times

in the bedroom (as part of saying goodbye rather than building a future). Especially if your partner is 'with' the third party but sneaking away to have sex with you, I would think again.

- If you have moved through all the previous points without coming up against an obstacle, but are still filled with doubt, you should consider couple-counselling.

Building up your confidence again

This exercise is especially for people whose partner has not been co-operative in the recovery process but can benefit anyone:

1. *Remember nobody is perfect.* Everyone does things that they regret. Think about a friend or family member: what good qualities and bad qualities does she or he have? Do his or her faults stop you from loving them? Could you offer the same compassion towards yourself?

2. *Be thankful for what you've got.* When we are about to lose something precious or fear losing it, this thing becomes so desirable that it eclipses everything else. So make a list of other valuable things in your life: children, family members, interesting job, etc.

3. *Identify your skills.* What are you good at? What personal qualities do other people value? Try and write down five things. If this is hard, ask your friends for suggestions.

4. *Accept compliments gracefully.* Partly because our parents told us 'pride comes before a fall' and partly because the playground is ruthless to anyone who stands out, we tend to downplay our achievements. So when someone compliments our clothes, we say 'this old thing' or if someone at work praises our handling of a complex problem, we say 'it was nothing'. Next time, accept the compliment gracefully with a thank-you.

5. *Stick to your principles.* When trying to rescue a relationship, many people turn themselves inside out to accommodate their partner. However, this can involve us accepting things that go against our core values and we end up feeling bad about ourselves. Drawing a line in the sand, and not stepping over, is an important step in recovering your confidence.

6. *Help others.* Doing something nice for other people is one of the best ways of feeling good about yourself.

7. *Set yourself a new challenge.* Make the goal something just outside your comfort zone and achieving it will be a major boost to your confidence.

8. *Fake it.* Until you are ready to be truly confident, pretend, and before too long you will be doing it for real.

Checkpoint

Three key points for dealing with Diversions, Derailments and Dead-Ends

1. There will be setbacks along the road to recovery. This is normal and does not mean your relationship is doomed.
2. If your self-respect is being destroyed by fighting to save a relationship against the odds, it is better to make a strategic retreat rather than plough on regardless.
3. Keep an open mind and do not be blinkered into seeking only the 'perfect' solution.

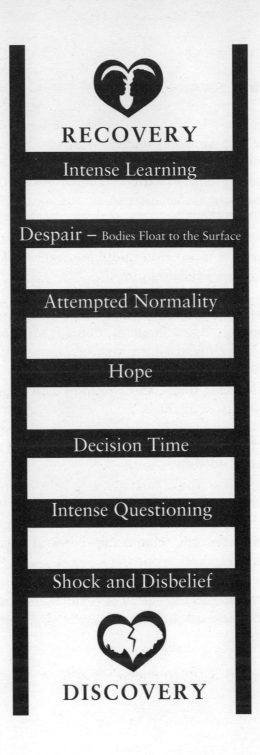

RECOVERY

Intense Learning

Despair – Bodies Float to the Surface

Attempted Normality

Hope

Decision Time

Intense Questioning

Shock and Disbelief

DISCOVERY

Infidelity: the seven lessons

1. Infidelity is completely destabilising. However, once discovered it provides an opportunity to put a relationship back together in a way that not only makes it better but, also, ultimately more satisfying.

2. Really listen to one another and understand where each of you is coming from. Don't hold anything back but at the same time don't yell and scream.

3. Don't make any quick decisions. There will be setbacks but, with patience, these can be overcome and your relationship put back on the road to recovery.

4. During the dark times, stay around positive people. You can learn to trust again.

5. It is better to hear the truth, however painful, than to be told sweet lies. (If the Discovered is determined to continue contact with the third party, let him or her go. The affair will more than likely self-destruct. However, it is extremely hard for your relationship to survive if your partner has promised to end the relationship but is discovered to be still unfaithful.)

6. The aftermath of an affair provides the opportunity, determination and focus to completely overhaul your relationship.

7. Forgiveness is a gift to yourself and frees you for a better tomorrow.

Acknowledgements

Thanks for the advice, help and support while I've been writing this book: Richard Atkinson, Natalie Hunt, Anya Rosenberg, Marian Reid, Ignacio Jarquin, Gail Louw, Jamie MacKay, Sherrell Pit-Kennedy, Chris Taylor, Vanessa Gebbie, Catherine Grace, Debby Edwards and all my clients and interviewees who contributed to my research.

A Note on the Author

Andrew G. Marshall is a marital therapist with RELATE, the UK's leading counselling charity, and writes regularly for newspapers and magazines around the world. He also runs workshops and gives talks on love and relationships. His other books include *I Love You But I'm Not in Love with You: Seven Steps to Saving Your Relationship* and *The Single Trap: The Two-step Guide to Escaping It and Finding Lasting Love* (both published by Bloomsbury). His work has been translated into fifteen languages.

www.andrewgmarshall.com